The Jewish Revolt

A Warsaw Ghetto Exhibition

Toby

THE JEWISH BRAND

Rachel Auerbach

THE JEWISH REVOLT

A Warsaw Ghetto Exhibition

TRANSLATED FROM YIDDISH BY

Michael Wex

The Jewish Brand
The Toby Press

The Jewish Revolt
A Warsaw Ghetto Exhibition

First Edition, 2025

The Toby Press
An imprint of Koren Publishers Jerusalem Ltd.

POB 8531, New Milford, CT 06776-8531, USA
& POB 4044, Jerusalem 9104001, Israel
www.korenpub.com

Book design: Stephen Morris, www.stephen-morris.co.uk

The publication of this book was made possible through
the generous support of *The Jewish Book Trust.*

ISBN 978-1-59264-697-5, *hardcover*

Printed and bound in the United States

This book is dedicated to:

The men and women
who fought together
and died together
fighting Fascism

CONTENTS

Warsaw, September 1946: Rachel Auerbach and Hirsch Wasser unearth the buried *Oyneg Shabes* archives

Foreword

I am writing this just five weeks after the events of October 7, 2023 with tears running down my cheeks. While the story of the Warsaw Ghetto, so poignantly recorded by Rachel Auerbach, has always been a key part of our Jewish history – a story of brave rebellion and ultimate devastation – for me it has never felt so relevant.

Once again, we have seen the mass slaughter of Jewish people. And we now understand that, just as people have always wanted to deny the events of the Holocaust, today – even as Hamas recorded their crimes and put them on the internet – there are people who will not believe what happened. Suddenly it is clear why Rachel and her colleagues were so intent on documenting everything that happened in the Ghetto; they knew they had to tell the story as clearly as they could so people would believe it.

Rachel, who had been a successful Polish- and Yiddish-speaking journalist before Hitler's invasion in 1939, felt the need to chronicle all those who were lost. Her story Yizker – named after the memorial service for deceased relatives – is a staggeringly tender portrait of a lost tribe. She is determined to try and remember each of them as they were marched out of the ghetto in deportations to, what she was later to discover, the gas chambers. From the beggars to the babies, the musicians to the bakers, the professors to the thieves, she wants to memoralise them all.

Her words are so heartfelt, in a few sentences she brings them back to life: the toddlers playing 'peek-a-boo', the beauty of the young women, the grandmothers, the mothers. She ensures that they are seen not just as bodies in mass graves, or numbers that make up the six million, but she draws them as individuals, gives them a flavour and a colour. She depicts them in all their humanity, killed for the single thing that united them: they are Jewish. She writes not as a historian but a journalist, as a woman, who sees as much importance in the market traders as the doctors and academics.

The story reminds me of a recent trip to Auschwitz. For me one of the most emotional places was the room filled with videos of Jewish life in all different parts of Europe before the genocide of the Nazis wiped it out. All those happy faces, shot, murdered, gassed, burnt.

The number six million is so hard to contemplate, but we must remember that each of them existed.

Those Rachel chronicled in Yizker included her niece, her cousins, her aunts. But, she writes, everyone who was marched to their death was her family; 'They are all mine, all my people – everybody who was killed.'

Brave Rachel, who was one of the last surviving members of the *Oyneg Shabes*. When the ghetto was established, its founder Emanuel Ringelblum, had gathered together a group of writers, historians and journalists to tell the story of what had happened – 'the recording angels' – so that the story would live on.

The idea was to 'bear witness' to the life and the death of the people of the ghetto, to examine the hunger, the cruelty and the eventual destruction. It was known that the Nazis would have their own story of what they had done; it was imperative to record every element of the truth.

As they faced almost certain death they knew they had no choice; in her work you can palpably feel the desperation to document it all so that one day people would remember.

As she spoke fluent Polish and could pass as a non-Jew, Rachel was sent out of the ghetto to help hide the documents – thousands of pieces of paper. She tells the story of the resistance, of her friends and her colleagues and their brave fight against an unstoppable force.

When the war was over, she helped retrieve most of the papers. Subsequently, she spent her life in Holocaust education: writing, working at Yad Vashem, ensuring the story of the ordinary people, the testimony of everyone, was recorded. Her passion to remember took over her life. As she wrote in Yizker:

> And should I forget for even a single day how I saw you, our desperate and forlorn people, consigned to extermination, may my name be forgotten. And my memory cursed like that of the traitors among us. Who are not worthy of a share in your pain.

I feel blessed to share a first name with Rachel Auerbach. I feel blessed to have been asked to write the foreword in this first English translation of such an important document. 'Never Again' has been the mantra of telling the story of the Holocaust and today, as I write this, the command feels ever more urgent.

She was only one Rachel, I am only another Rachel, but the fight to remember, and this fight against antisemitism, is one we can all play our part in. As this book shows, individuals can make a difference, especially when they combine against oppression.

Rachel Riley

Rachel Riley is a TV presenter and campaigner against antisemitism. She was awarded an MBE for Services to Holocaust Education

Photo Essay: Yellow Star

From Life to Destruction

Radomsk, Poland 1929: Wilhelm Maniak in a studio photograph

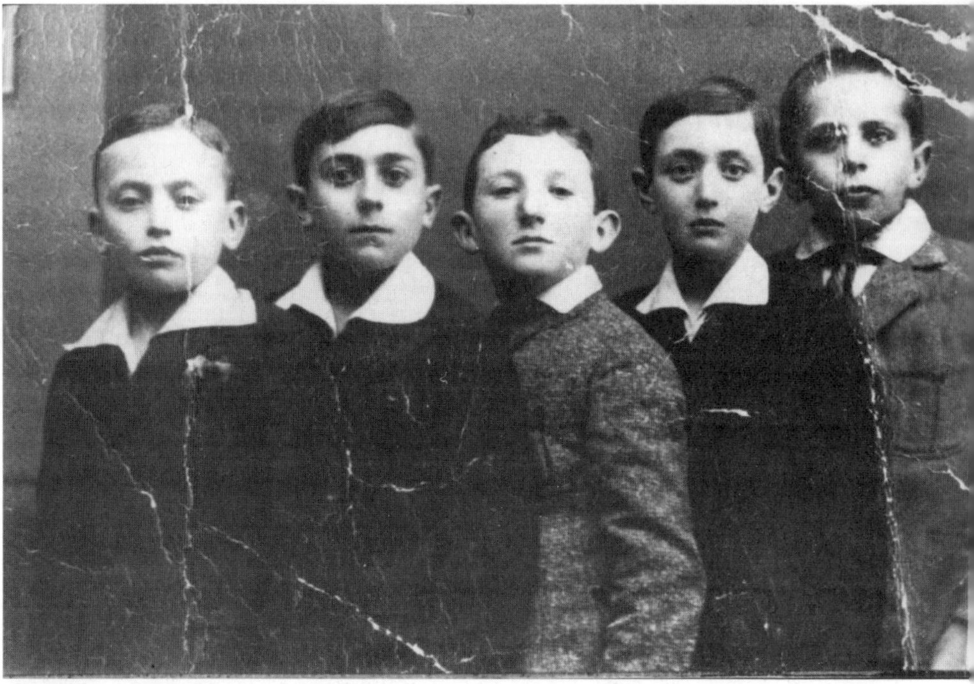

Podwoloczyska, Poland: five friends, Motel Helman, Moshe Sigal, Dov Brayer, Izio Halperin and Shaye Barenboim. Dov Brayer – centre – was the only one to survive

Lublin 1937: Henio Żytomirski and Ester Rechtman

Litewski Square (?) Lublin, 1936: Henio and his mother Sarą Żytomirska

Grodno, Poland, 1934: the Pinski children

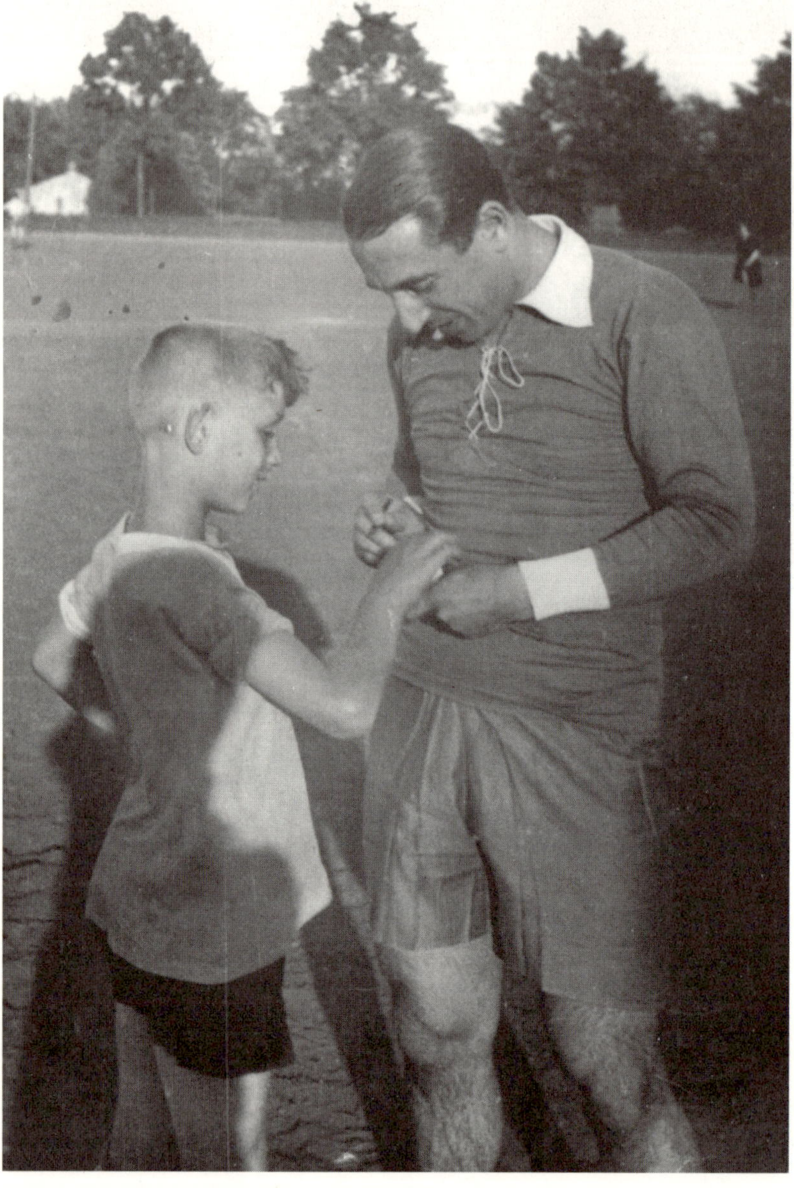

Berlin, 1930: the Jewish tennis player Daniel Pren of the Bar-Kochba movement

France, 1937: a Jewish football team

Breslau, Germany, 1922: the Alpert family

Breslau, Germany, 1927: children of the Alpert family

Above and below: persons currently unknown, circa 1930 found in Lublin, Poland

Rozyszcze, Poland, 1938: Frida Pleben with her uncle Shlomo Grebelski

Persons currently unknown, circa 1930: Lublin (?), Poland

Nalewki Street Warsaw, 1939

Person currently unknown, Lublin (?) Poland, circa 1930

Person currently unknown, Lublin (?) Poland, circa 1930

Person currently unknown, Lublin (?) Poland, circa 1930

Persons currently unknown, Lublin (?) Poland, circa 1930

Berlin, 1932

Germany, 1940: the wedding of a member of the Arieh Hendler family

Bielsko-Biala, Poland, January 1937: Stefan Altheim dressed for bar mitzvah

Thessaloniki, Greece,1936: Into Shymshi's bar mitzvah ceremony

Work

Warsaw (1941?): hat making at 28 Nalewki Street

Lublin, Poland: a tailor's shop circa 1930

Warsaw (1941?), sewing at 28 Nalewki Street

Lublin (?) Poland circa 1930: a tailor listening to his radio

Opposite and above: persons currently unknown, circa 1930, found Lublin, Poland

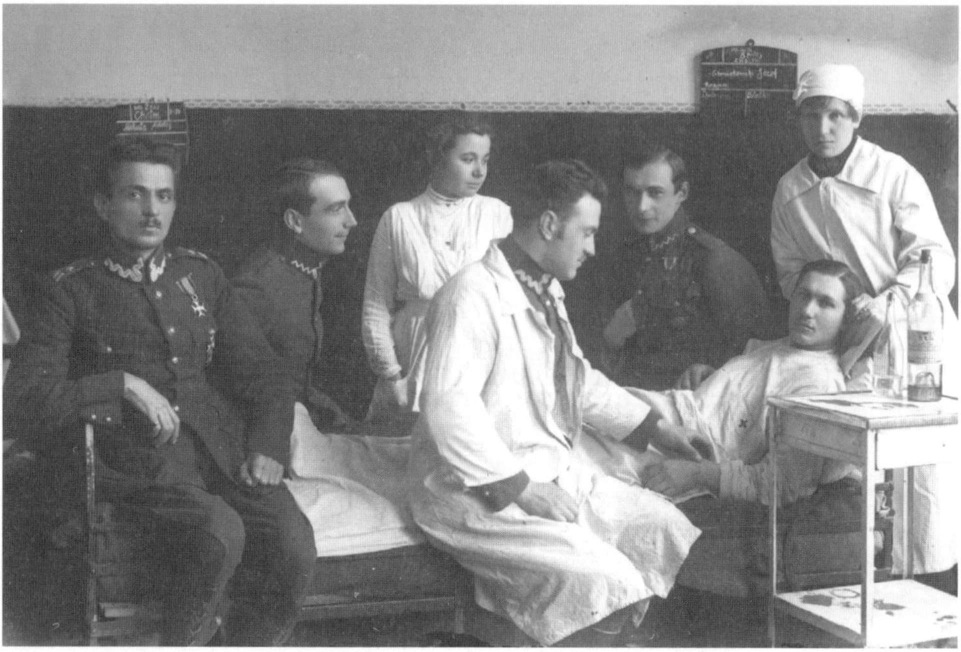

Chelm, Poland, circa 1930: a hospital

Germany 1933

Nuremberg

Nuremberg and Dortmund

Berlin, 1933: SA members enforcing a boycott of a shop in Jewish ownership

The burning of books by *Deutsche Studentenschaft*, May 1933

Presov, Slovakia, 1942: identifying a Jewish business

The Yellow Star

Birkenau

Lodz Ghetto, Poland: Marian Kleiman in his office

Belgium: currently unknown bride and groom

The aftermath of *Kristallnacht*, 9 to 10 November 1938

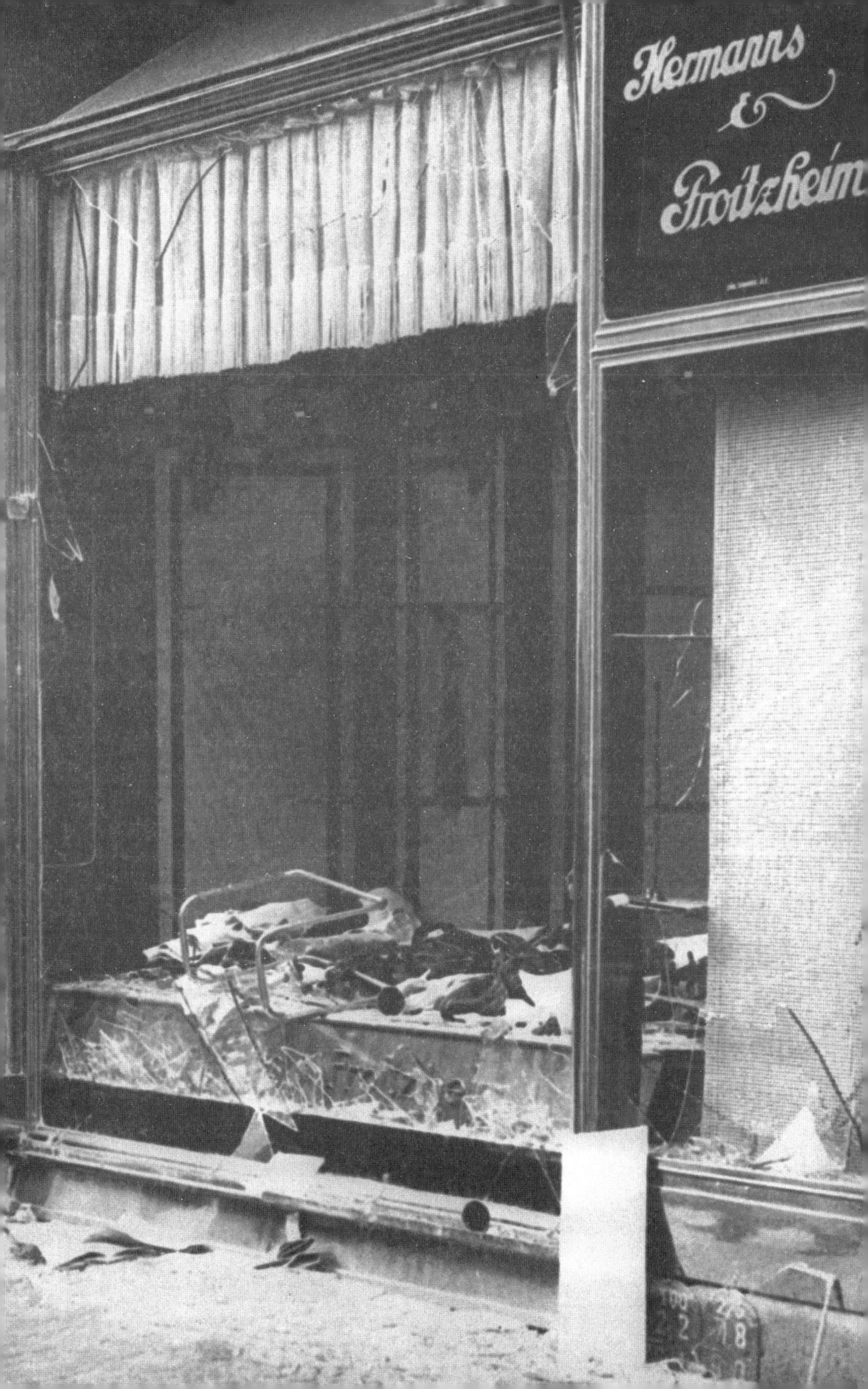
Hermanns
&
Froitzheim

Trzebina, Poland, 1940: Jachelt Melzer

Germany invades Poland, 1939

Warsaw, a synagogue burns

Warsaw 1939: Pasaz Simonsa at the beginning of Nalewki Street

Warsaw 1939: destroyed buildings in the market by the Iron Gate

Sanok, Poland, September 1939: Jews rounded up for forced labour

The Ghetto

Building the walls

Building the walls

The bridge on Chlodna St connecting the two parts of ghetto. Aryan Warsaw is below

A Jews-only tram in the Ghetto.
Jewish police on traffic duty

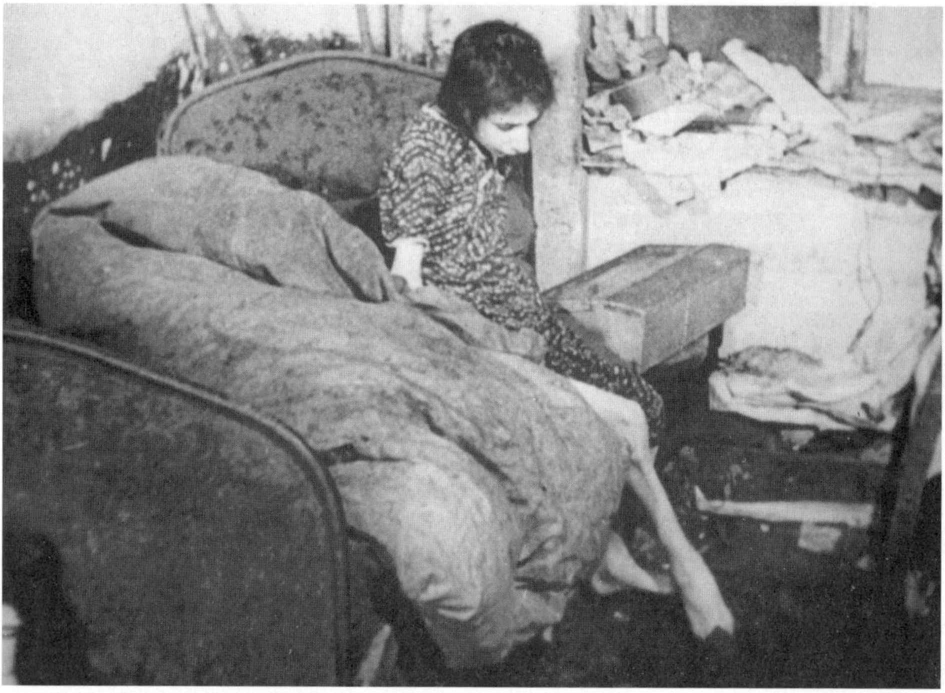

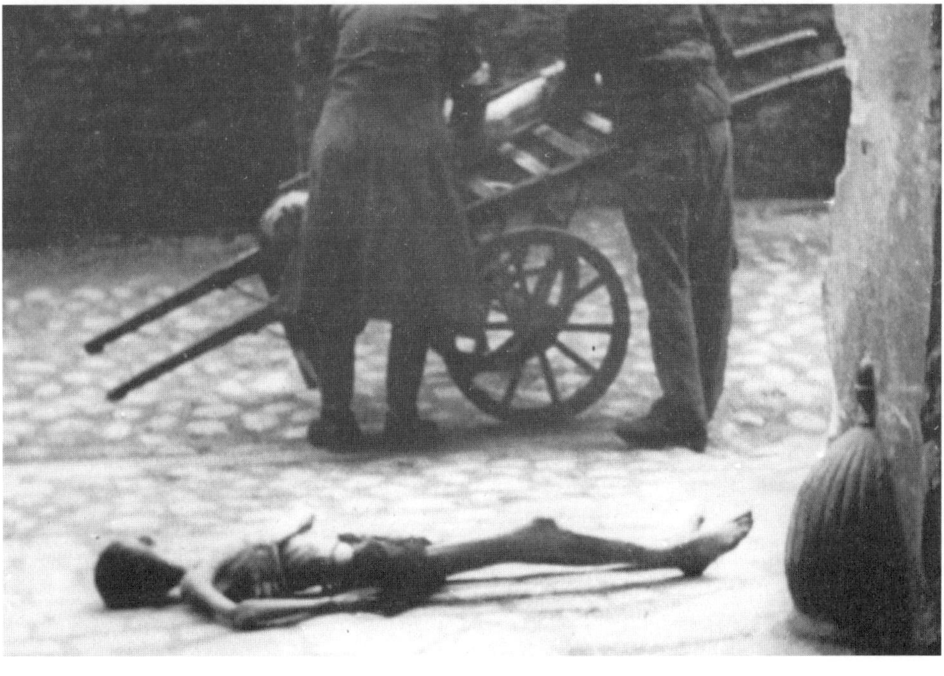

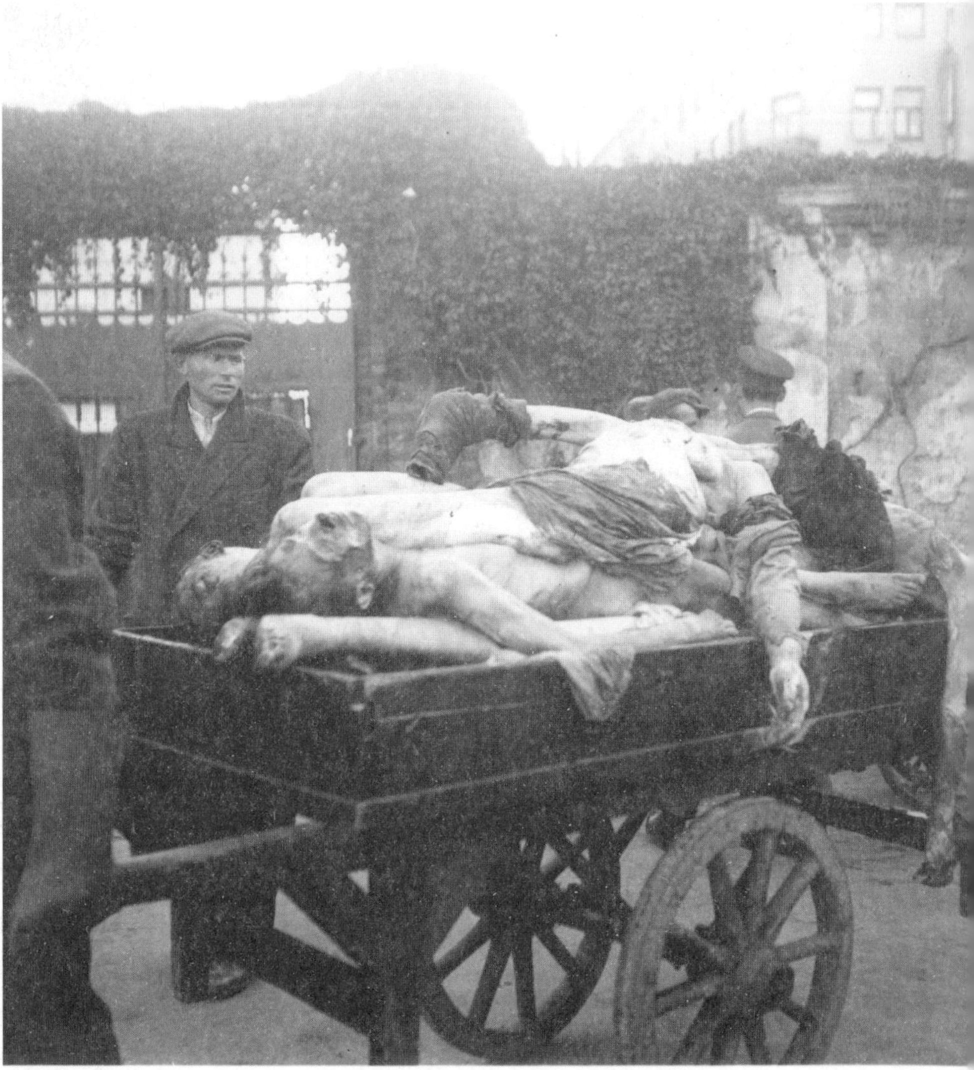

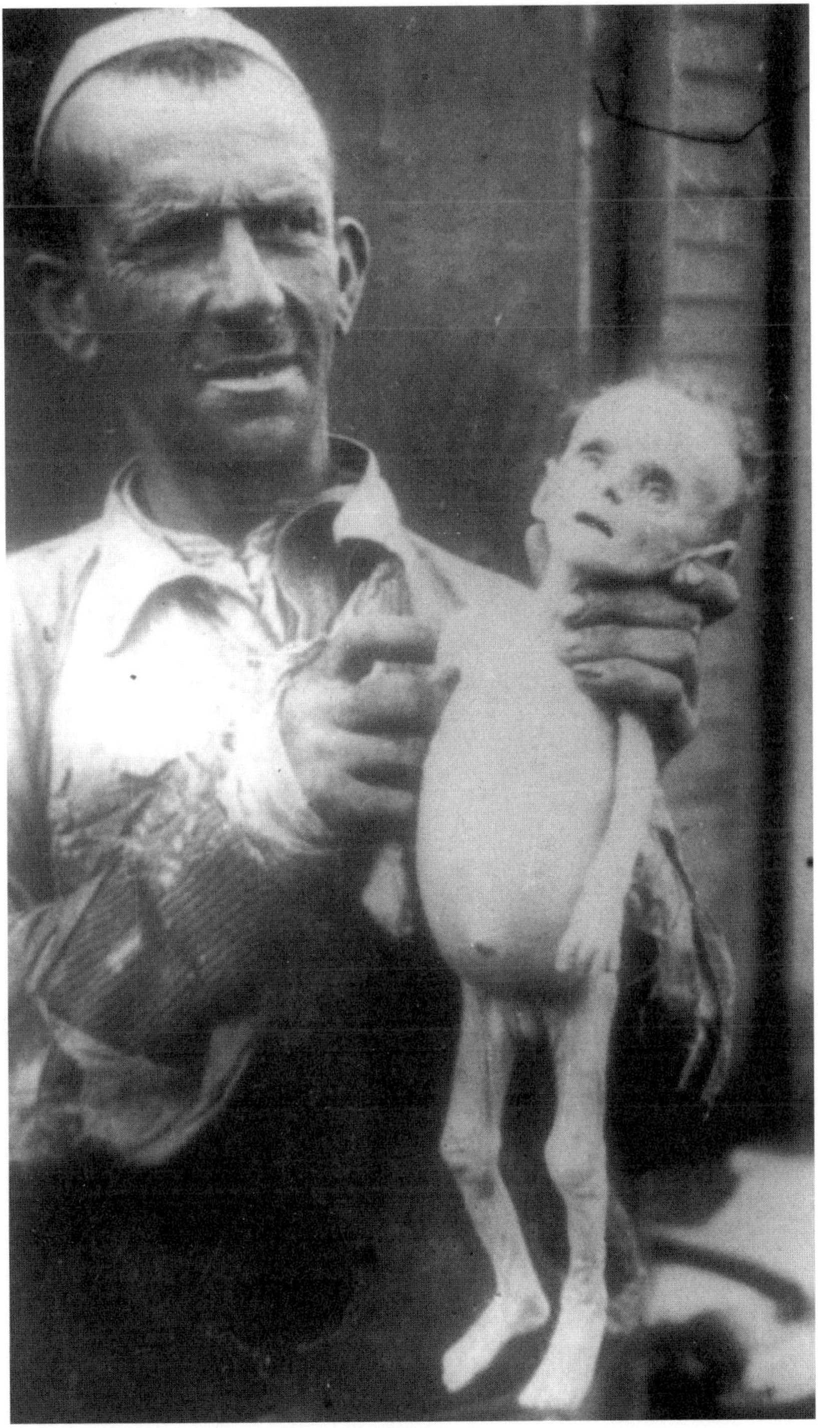

Rachel Auerbach

YIZKER 1943
(Remember)
(written on the Aryan side of Warsaw, 1943)

I saw a flood in the mountains once.

Wooden cottages uprooted in the middle of the night bounced wildly on the furious river's waves, lamps still burning inside; men and women, children in cradles lashed to the rafters with ropes.

Other huts, already empty, had tangles of hands growing out of their roofs. Fluttering like branches in a storm, desperately wringing, reaching vainly for help from the sky or the shore. Wide-open mouths could be seen from afar, but the roar of the waters drowned any screams.

So did the Jewish masses flow to their deaths in the days of the deportation. They sank just as helplessly in the flood of utter destruction.

*

And should I forget for even a single day how I saw you, our desperate and forlorn people, consigned to extermination, may my name be forgotten.

And my memory cursed like that of the traitors among us.

Who are not worthy of a share in your pain.

*

Every inborn instinct of the multitude was uncovered. Every feeling stirred up and inflamed to its core, driven on by hundreds of whips of furious activity, hundreds of clever ideas for supposed rescue schemes. And the other side of the coin – surrender to the inevitable, an urge to mass death as real as the urge to live. Both in the same soul at times, either successively or at once.

Who can describe the stages of mass extinction, beyond the shudder of pity for oneself and others? The same mirages and delusions all over again: the wait for sudden miracles, the unhinged smile of hope in the eyes of the terminally ill, the ghostly play of colours on the waxy-yellow face of someone sentenced to death.

Sentenced to death! Who can conceive it? Who would want to? How were simple Jews, the lower branches of the Jewish tree, the little plants of the world – how were the Jewish masses – to prepare for this decree?

People who would have lived their lives untroubled by the justice – or even the injustice – of the world.

How were such people, who were like children at the dentist, pale with fear at having a tooth pulled – how were these people supposed to get ready to die in a gas chamber?

And what about the little children?

And the littler and the littlest, still cradled in their mothers' arms, smiling at a bird or a sunbeam, playing peek-a-boo with strangers on the tram. Children who were still playing patty-cake, yelling "Giddyup," and gesturing with their little hands: "Eat, eat."

Eat, eat! What kind of world is this? The children and their mothers all gone "giddyup"...

Together with the sweet two-and three-year-olds, rolling around like newly hatched chicks on their dainty little legs. And the slightly older ones who were already talking, who never stop asking what words mean and learning everything for the very first time. Children five, six, seven years old. And the bigger ones, their eyes wide with curiosity about everything in the world. And those whose eyes were already veiled with the fog of adolescence...Boys whose games were preparing them for future deeds.

Girls nursing dolls in the corner, with great cockades on their heads, leaping about like sparrows in the courtyards and garden paths.

And those like half-open blossoms already, their cheeks brushed by a glowing caress of the first wind of spring – girls of eleven and twelve, thirteen-year-olds with the faces of angels – playful kittens, the smiling flowers of May.

And those about to bloom. The fourteen-, fifteen-, and sixteen-year-olds. The Sarahs and Rebeccas, Rachels and Leahs of the Bible – but with Polish nicknames; eyes of blue and green under the arched brows of Egyptian and Babylonian murals; slender young ladies from the wells of Hebron, maidens from the Gospels. The exotic concubines of Hebrew patriarchs, desert maids with flaring nostrils, curly hair, and dusky skin, wan with the heat of their blood...Daughters of Spain, lady loves of medieval Hebrew poets – dreamy flowers curving over the surface of the water. And you delicate blondes, equal parts Hebrew ardour and Slavic gaiety. And even fairer girls of cornsilk and flax, wide-hipped peasants who can be likened to black bread or a homespun shirt on the body of the nation.

There was something eerie about the overabundance of beauty among girls of a generation growing up against the grey backdrop of ghetto poverty and mass hunger. How did we fail to notice so ominous a sign? How did we fail to see this blooming as a portent of our end?

And they went down into the abyss, our beautiful daughters, they were swept away and devoured!

And where are the young Jewish boys? Serious and severe, fiery, like pedigreed young horses chomping at the bit and yearning to run. Young workers, *khalutsim*, Jewish students with a passion for learning, for sports, for politics; reformers, standard-bearers for every revolution, ready in their ardour to fill all the prison cells on earth. Many of them were tortured in the camps even before the mass-murder began.

And other, more ordinary boys, the down-to-earth roots of a people with its head in the clouds, a tincture of sobriety to balance the idealistic degeneration of the race.

Young men in whom the sap was rising, their bulls' heads thrust forward as if to gore, their necks as stiff as iron at the sentence pronounced on our people.

Pious Jews in black capotes, looking for all the world like priests in their medieval garb, rabbis and scholars who wanted to transform our whole lives into Torah study and prayer to God. They were the first to feel the murderers' wrath. They didn't talk about martyrdom all the time for nothing...

And still other Jews – broad-shouldered, husky voiced, with rugged strength in their hearts and hands, artisans, workers. Teamsters and porters who could flatten any hooligan who dared invade their turf with a single blow of their fist.

Where were you when they took your wives and children, your aged parents? What happened to make you run into the fire like oxen? Were you carried off by the flood with those who were weaker than you because there was no one to show you a way out of the panic?

And you merchants from Nalewki St., cunning, shrewd, in cut-off frock coats and caps, how did you fail to recognize the deadly fraud? Warsaw patriarchs and matriarchs, broad-beamed businesswomen among mountains of merchandise behind the cash-desks of their stores, big, strong faces glowing with wisdom over their three-fold double-chins.

And you other mothers. Toil-weary market women – as disheveled and terrified as angry brood hens flapping their wings in fiery concern for their young.

Other fathers, who have already hung up their spurs, selling candy and saccharin from wobbly tables in the ghetto.

It is a kind of mania, this desire to list every kind of Jew who was killed!

Grandmothers and grandfathers flecked with grandchildren. With white heads and hands like withered leaves, trembling over a life that was already over. They were not fated to go down to their graves weary and anxious for rest, like a day declining into the great ocean's waves. It was decreed that they see the ruin of everything that had come forth from them, the destruction of everything they had built.

The decree on the children and elderly was crueler, more total, than the others.

*

...The worthy and the less worthy. Those with aptitudes honed in the toil and torment of countless generations. Incomparable talents with treasure troves of deep and specialized knowledge – great and prominent doctors, professors, musicians, painters, architects.

And Jews from the manual trades –

Tailors, renowned and in demand – golden Jewish hands! Jewish watchmakers, the only ones the gentiles trusted! Jewish carpenters, printers, bakers – Warsaw's huge Jewish proletariat! Should I console myself with the thought that most of you managed to die of hunger and want in the ghetto before you could be deported?

*

O, the Warsaw way of life, the black, Jewish earth of Warsaw – a vast reservation!

My heart even weeps for the lowest thief on Krochmalna and the worst cut-throat from narrow Mila Street. Because they, too were killed for being Jewish, cleansed and anointed in a common grave.

O, where are you, you jolly petty thieves, you "choir boys" and dealers in rotten fruit? And you bigger malefactors, members of larger gangs that convened their own rabbinic courts, had their own synagogues on the High Holidays, held solemn funerals and distributed charity like the most respectable bourgeois householders.

O, madmen of the Jewish streets, crazed wartime jesters!

O, bagel ladies on winter evenings!

O impoverished children of the ghetto, ghetto traders, little ghetto smugglers, providing for their families, courageous and faithful to the last. Poor barefoot boys with boxes of cigarettes in the autumn slush.

"Cigarettes, cigarettes! Matches, matches!" The voice of the little cigarette seller at the corner of Leszno and Karmelicka still rings in my ears.

Where are you, little boy? What did they do with you?

A ribbon of film from a pre-deportation movie that was never shot and has yet to be shown keeps spooling and unspooling in my memory. It's called *The Singing Ghetto*, a movie where even dead people sing. They beg and stamp their swollen feet:

Mues, mues	Money, money
Mues iz di beste zakh	Money is the best thing.*

No power, no ill-omened hour could crush this struggle for Jewish existence.

* To the tune of the Tin-Pan Alley standard, "Ja-Da" (translator's note).

Until the day of wrath arrived – a day that was one long night...*

Hitler had finally achieved his greatest wartime victory.

His most prominent enemy had fallen in defeat – the little boy from the corner of Leszno and Karmelicka, Smocza and Nowolipie, from Dzika Street.

All the market women unsheathed their weapons: "Big spender's got a shopping bag!"

They stopped screaming their throats raw from morning to night and snatching one another's bits of clay-yellow bread, baked with clay in the flour and cut into quarters with the knife of privation.

*

The beggars were the first to be taken. The jobless and homeless were all cleared from the streets. They were loaded into wagons on the first day of the deportations and driven through the city. They wailed and reached their hands out, wrung them in despair or used them to hide their faces.

"Mama!" cried the youngest. "Mama!"

You could see women running on either side of the carts, their kerchiefs sliding off their heads, clambering up to their children, the underage smugglers who had been cleared from the ghetto wall.

The captives in the other wagons looked like old engravings of condemned prisoners in a tumbril bound for the gallows.

The wailing died down, went mute. No more lamenting was heard in the days that followed. The occasional hiss, perhaps, like that of hens for the slaughter, as women were seized and loaded forcibly onto the wagons.

Most of the men were silent. Even the children rarely raised a cry of terror.

*The first Aktion (Deportation) took place July 22, 1942.

Only once did I hear singing during the deportation, a Yiddish song with a monotonous tune from the steppes, sung by a beggar girl of thirteen. For about two weeks, she would crawl out of her hideout every day at evening when the deportations stopped, then, pale and tall, with an ever-larger halo of sorrow around her head...she would take up her old station in front of a building on Leszno, and warble her trills for a piece of bread.

No, no. I can't stop. I recall another girl, about fourteen. My own brother's orphaned daughter from Lviv, whom I used to carry around as if she were my own. Lucia! And another, older Lucia, a cousin of mine who was studying in Lviv and whom I thought of as a younger sister. And the first Lucia's mother, my brother's widow Łonia and her oldest child, who had been like a son to me since he was orphaned – Mundek. And another girl from my family, the thirteen-year-old pianist, my talented little cousin Josima.*

And all the brood from my mother's side in the far-off Podolian village: Aunt Beyle, Aunt Tsirl, Uncle Jasia and Aunt Dorcia, my childhood ideal of beauty – Auntie Dorcia...

So many names to mention! How can I leave any out when almost all of them have gone off to Belzeć and Treblinka or were killed on the spot in Lanovice and Jezierzany, in Chortkiv and Mielnica, in Krzywcza and everywhere else.

Absurd! I won't mention any more names. They are all mine, all my people – everybody who was killed. But those whom I knew and loved take up all the space in my memory, which today is a sort of burial ground – the only memorial to their time on earth.

*

*Josima Feldschuh, 1929-1943, a prodigy who gave at least one concert in the Warsaw Ghetto and whose compositions continue to be featured in programs dedicated to music of the Holocaust (trans.).

Josima Feldshuh

Mundik Meir and Lusya Tsirl Oyerbakh

I know and feel that this is what they want...Every day I mention another one of those who are gone.

And when, one by one, I get to the end of the series during another one of my errands in the city, I start all over again. They are painful, these names, each in its own way, like body parts that have been operated on, hands and feet that have been amputated, every missing finger and toe, thanks to the nerves still left in my system.

Not long ago I ran into a woman on the tram, talking to herself with her head thrown back. I thought she was drunk or mentally ill. But she was a mother who had just got news that her son who had been picked up on the street, had been shot.

"My child!" she stammered, paying no attention to the other passengers, "my son, most beautiful in the world."

I would have wanted to talk to myself too, like a madwoman, a drunk, like the woman in the Book of Judges* who poured her heart out to God and was driven from the Tabernacle by the high priest Eli.

I may not groan and I may not cry. I may not call attention to myself on the street.

And I have to cry so badly, have to groan. Not four times a year, but four times a day I want to say *Yizkor*.

*

Yizkor...Remember, O Lord, the souls of all those dear to me who departed this world before their time in frightening, unnatural deaths.

And suddenly I see myself as a child, standing on a bench behind my mother, who is praying by the eastern wall of the women's section of the Lanovice synagogue along with my grandmother.

I am standing on tiptoe and looking down through the lattice at the men in the synagogue that my grandfather built. And now Meyer-Itzik Hersh, the Torah reader, raps the lectern three times and calls out in a mighty voice that can be heard by women and women on either side of the divider, that will reach the orphan girls and boys who are standing and waiting for him to call out:

"Time for *Yizkor*."

The solemn moment in memory of those who are no more has come. Even people who no longer pray but come at such times to be with the others are waiting for the announcement:

"Time for *Yizkor*."

*Actually 1 Samuel, chapter 1 (trans.)

And let any survivor who comes there hang his head and listen to the pain in her heart and mention their names, as I have mentioned mine. The names of those who were killed.

At the end of the prayer into which everyone inserts the names of their own relatives, there is a verse in memory of those who were visited at various times with violent deaths because they were Jews and have no one left to remember them.

Today they are a majority.

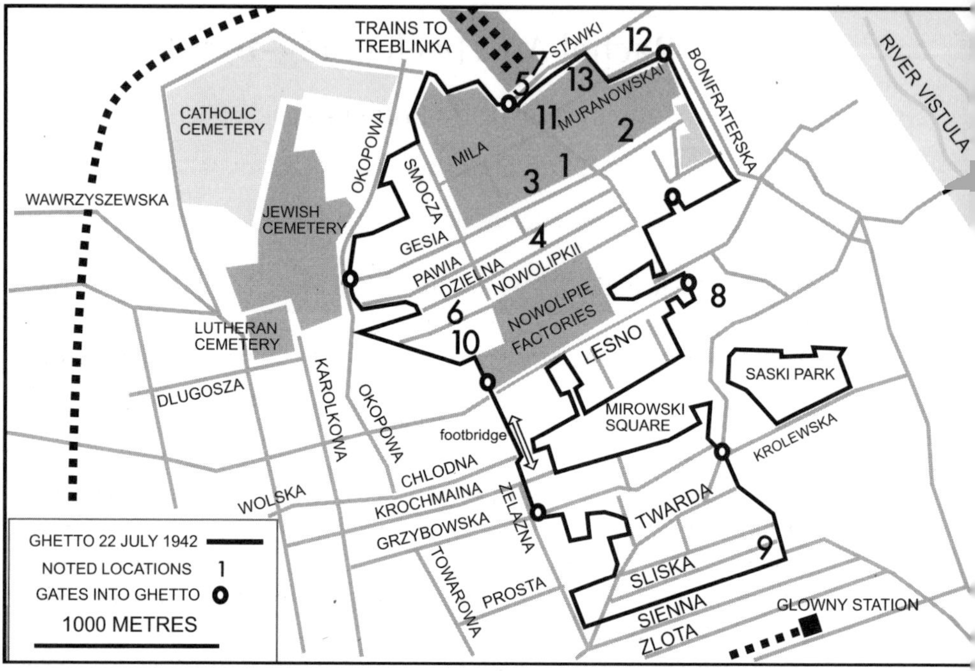

The Ghetto, July 1942

1 Judenrat
2 Jewish Police
3 Gesiowka Prison
4 Pawiak Prison
5. Assembley point and Transfer Office
6 Ringelblum archive hidden here
7 Czyste Hosp. Deportation Centre
8 Great Synagogue
9 Korczak Orphanage
10 Deportation Office
11 ZOB HQ
12 ZZW HQ
13 SS Werterfassung

Rachel Auerbach (1903-1976)

Antony Polonsky

Rachel Auerbach, author of 'Yizker 1943', a moving elegy for Warsaw Jewry written during the war and *Der Yidisher Oyfshtand: Varshe 1943* (*The Jewish Uprising: Warsaw 1943*), a vivid account of the Warsaw Ghetto Uprising of April-May 1943, published in Yiddish in Warsaw in 1948, which form the core of this book, produced a large corpus of work on the fate of the Jews under Nazi occupation. Almost none of this has been translated into English[1] and there is thus all the more reason to welcome this volume which makes available to an English-speaking audience the work of this important writer, who also organized soup kitchens in the Warsaw ghetto and later played an important role in the *Oyneg Shabes*, the ghetto's underground archive organized by Emanuel Ringelblum.

Auerbach was born in Łanowce (today Lanovitsy in Ukraine), a small village in Podolia, where her rural childhood imbued her with a deep knowledge and affection for popular Yiddish culture. She studied psychology and philosophy at the University of Lwów and became active as a journalist in both Polish and Yiddish, collaborating with the poet and essayist Melech Ravitch in the journal *Tsushtayer,* which sought to promote Yiddish culture in the unpromising environment of Galicia, where the autonomy granted to the Polish rulers of the province from the 1860s had led to the adoption of policies which favoured Jewish acculturation. As a result, the bulk of the Jewish intelligentsia here adopted the Polish language.

In 1933 Auerbach moved to Warsaw where she wrote extensively on literature, theatre and psychology in the Polish-language Jewish newspaper *Nasz Przegląd* and in the Yiddish press. She had a stormy relationship with the Yiddish poet Itsik Manger, which effectively ended when Manger, a Romanian citizen, was forced to leave Poland in 1938. The two remained in contact and Auerbach subsequently hid many of his manuscripts in the secret Ringelblum archive which was buried in July-August 1942 and February 1943.

After the outbreak of war in 1939, she intended to return to Lwów but the

1 Only 'Yizker' has been published in English in David Roskies (ed.), *The Literature of Destruction: Jewish Responses to Catastrophe* (Philadelphia, 1988), 459-464.

historian Emanuel Ringelblum, whose views were close to hers both in their radicalism and their belief in the importance of Yiddish, persuaded her to organize soup kitchens in Warsaw and subsequently in the Warsaw Ghetto. Two years later, he also invited her to join the *Oyneg Shabes*, the secret underground archive he had established and to write an account of the functioning of the soup kitchen at 40 Leszno Street, which fed 2,000 Jews a day. This had provided her with a unique vantage point to observe the desperate struggle to survive which marked ghetto life. She soon began to doubt whether the soup kitchen could actually alleviate the conditions of starvation to which the Jews were subjected, asking on 4 August 1941 in her diary, which she kept in Polish and which has been published in Yiddish as *Baym Letstn Veg: In Geto Varshe un oyf der Arisher Zayt* (*On the Last Journey: In the Warsaw Ghetto and on the Aryan Side*, Tel Aviv, 1977), 'What is the use of all of our work if we can't save even one person from death by hunger?'

She also, at Ringelblum's request, recorded the testimony of Avrom (Yankev) Krzepicki, an escapee from the Treblinka death camp, who was able to return to the Warsaw Ghetto in September 1942. His testimony was one of the first to confirm that the nearly a quarter of a million Jews who were deported from the ghetto in the summer of 1942 had not been sent to work in the east, as they had been told by the Nazis, but had been murdered in Treblinka.

In March 1943 Auerbach escaped to the 'Aryan side' of Warsaw and was recruited by Adolf and Basia Berman as a courier for the underground Jewish National Committee they had set up. In hiding, she continued to write extensively both in Polish and Yiddish for the 'Arkhiv Hemshekh' ('The Continuing Archive', a reference to the work of *Oyneg Shabes*) – the underground Jewish archive on the Aryan side. With the help of Polish friends, she buried her writings in two different locations in Warsaw, in the grounds of the Warsaw Zoo, where the director Jan Żabiński and his wife strongly supported her activity, and in a field in the southern district of Mokotów. Both caches survived the war. It was at this time that she wrote 'Yizker' in Yiddish.

When the war ended, Auerbach, one of only three survivors of the *Oyneg Shabes* group, was tireless in her insistence that the buried archive should be found and dug up. The Yiddish writer Mendel Mann recalled Auerbach's talk at the third anniversary commemoration of the ghetto uprising. After many rather tedious political speeches, Auerbach, the only woman on the podium, got up to speak:

> She did not make any speeches, she did not 'explain the meaning' of the uprising. She implored! With a stubbornness that deeply affected

The soup kitchen at 33 Nalewki Street fed 2,000 people a day

The equivalent daily calorific intake for Jews in the Ghetto: 184 calories

> me, she demanded, she called: Remember, she cried out, there is a national treasure under the ruins...Even if there are five stories of ruins, we have to find the archive. I'm not making this up. I know what I'm talking about! This isn't just talk! This is coming from my heart. I will not rest and I will not let you rest. We must rescue the Ringelblum archive![2]

It was, above all, thanks to her, that the remaining part of the archive was discovered and has been preserved in the Jewish Historical Institute in Warsaw.

From 1945 until 1950, she dedicated herself to documenting the fate of the Jews under Nazism in Poland. In November 1945 she was a member of a fact-finding mission to Treblinka conducted by the Polish State Committee for the Investigation of Nazi War Crimes on Polish Soil and published a report on functioning of the camp, *Oyf di Felder fun Treblinke* (*In the Fields of Treblinka*, Warsaw, 1947). In this she anticipated Jan Gross's observations in his book *Golden Harvest* (New York, 2012) in describing, in a chapter with the title 'The Polish Colorado or About the Gold Rush in Treblinka' how after the war, those who lived in the vicinity of Treblinka, whom she described as 'human jackals and hyenas', were searching the site of the camp in the hope of finding valuables brought there by the subsequently murdered Jews. She was a co-founder of the Central Jewish Historical Commission in Łódź and served as literary and history editor of its publication *Dos Naye Leben* (*The New Life*). She was one of the first to set out the guidelines for recording witness testimony and became part of the team in Poland which collected a large mass of survivor testimonies at the Jewish Historical Commission and its successor, the Jewish Historical Institute, which is one of the key tools for Holocaust research in Poland today. It was at this time she wrote *Der Yidisher Oyfshtand: Varshe 1943* (published in Warsaw in 1948). She wrote it in Yiddish, part of the vain effort to preserve this language, which had been largely destroyed by the Nazi mass murder of its speakers.

In 1950, distressed by the growing Stalinization of political life in Poland and the increasing politicization of Holocaust research, she emigrated to Israel with two other key figures in the Jewish Historical Institute, Yosef Kermish and Nachman Blumental. Here, after some delay, in March 1954 she was appointed Director of Yad Vashem's new Department for the Collection of Witness Testimony, located in Tel Aviv, where most Holocaust survivors who had emigrated to Israel had settled. She interviewed local survivors and attempted to compile a data base of those who survived. In her view, survivor

2 Mendel Mann, 'Rokhl Auerbach tsu ir bazukh in pariz', *Unzer vort*, 6 August 1966.

testimony was important in Holocaust research for three reasons. Firstly, the available Holocaust documentation largely originated from Nazi sources, which 'told only the story of the murderers, but not of the murdered'.[3] Witness testimony allowed researchers to understand Jewish lives during the Holocaust, not just the mechanics of Jewish deaths. Secondly, she saw these testimonies as therapeutic for the survivors, saying: 'I am convinced that the confessions, called giving testimony, from the era of the Holocaust have a calming and healing influence and help free them [the survivors] from the horrors'.[4] Third, she saw as an important goal the building up of a mass of documentation that could be used in future criminal trials of Nazis. She certainly gathered witness testimonies for the trial of Adolf Eichmann and personally testified at his trial. The Director of the Fortunoff Video Archive for Holocaust Testimonies Stephen Naron has observed that after a visit to Yad Vashem

> ... I received a copy of Oyerbakh's oral testimony guidelines, an 18-page Hebrew document drafted in 1962. ... When I read it, and this was no surprise to me really, it was so clear how her motivations for recording testimony, her methodology ... foreshadowed the work the Fortunoff Archive would start in New Haven in 1979.[5]

Her stress on survivor testimony led to a clash with the Directorate of Yad Vashem, headed by Ben-Zion Dinur, who saw Holocaust research in more instrumental terms as part of the struggle against contemporary antisemitism. This came to a head in 1957-8, and Auerbach was able successfully to defend her position. However, her situation in the organization was now much weaker and she was compelled to retire from her position when she turned 65 in 1968.[6] Her view on the nature of Holocaust research also led to a public dispute with the French author Jean-François Steiner in 1967 over his fictional account of the death camp in *Treblinka* (Paris, 1960).

Once established in Israel, Auerbach continued to write. She wrote one book, *Undzer Kheshbn mitn Daytshn Folk* (*Our Reckoning With the German People*, in Yiddish, Tel Aviv. 1952) in which she expressed her feelings of anger at the German war on the Jews. Above all, however, she now concentrated on memorializing the lost world of Polish, and particularly Warsaw, Jewry. This

3 Boaz Cohen, 'Rachel Auerbach, Yad Vashem and Holocaust Memory', *Polin: Studies in Polish Jewry*, vol 20 (Oxford and Portland, OR 2008), 199.
4 Ibid., 200.
5 Rokhl Kafrissen, 'Rokhl's Golden City: Rokhl Oyerbakh belatedly gains recognition for uncovering the truth about life in the Warsaw Ghetto', *Tablet*, 20 November 2019. Online at: https://www.tabletmag.com/tags/rokhl-oyerbakh
6 On this controversy, see Boaz Cohen, *Rachel Auerbach*, 197-221.

was the theme of *Behutsot Varsha 1939–1943* (*In the Streets of Warsaw 1939–1943*, in Hebrew, Tel Aviv, 1954). Her view of the Polish-Jewish past is most eloquently expressed in the series of sketches of Jewish cultural life, *Varshever Tsavoes: Bagegenishn, Aktivitetn, Goyroles, 1933–1945* (*Warsaw Testaments: Encounters, Activities, Fates 1933–1945* in Yiddish, Tel Aviv, 1974); translated into Hebrew as *Tzavaot varshah: Mifgashim, Maasim, Goralot* (Tel Aviv, 1985) and into English by Samuel Kassow as *Warsaw Testament* by Rokhl Auerbach (Amherst, MA, 2024).

There is a very significant difference in tone and emphasis between the way Auerbach treated Holocaust issues during the war and her writings after liberation. In all her work on the Jewish catastrophe, she was concerned to highlight the character of Warsaw Jewry and to document its leading role in the culture life of Polish Jewry. In the words of Samual Kassow:

> Jewish Warsaw was the largest Jewish community in Europe. It was a sprawling, intense, dynamic community whose Jewish population had skyrocketed from 40,000 in 1862 to 350,000 by the eve of World War II. Warsaw was a powerful magnet that attracted Jewish migrants from the Hasidic shtetls of central Poland, and Litvaks from Lithuania and White Russia.
>
> ...[At] the same time, its theatres, newspapers, cafes, publishing houses and libraries turned Warsaw into a cultural center for Jews and Poles. While the Poles showed no interest in Warsaw's thriving Yiddish culture, the city's Jews not only flocked to the Yiddish cultural institutions but were also often the most dependable patrons of Polish theater and literature. Unlike cities such as Vilna or Białystok, a significant proportion of Warsaw Jewry – especially the middle and professional classes – was Polish-speaking.
>
> And after Poland became an independent state, Jewish Warsaw took on a new role. It helped turn Jews from Galicia, Congress Poland and the Litvak Jews of the northeast borderlands into 'Polish Jews'.[7]

In the years before the outbreak of the war, Auerbach had been rather pessimistic about the future of Jewish Warsaw and, in particular, of its role as a Yiddish cultural centre. She even thought of leaving Poland, as had Itsik Manger. However, by 1939, she had become determined to remain there, writing to Melekh Ravitch that if Yiddish had any future, it was in Poland and

7 Samuel Kassow, 'The Warsaw Ghetto in the Writings of Rachel Auerbach', in Glenn Dynner and François Guesnet, *Warsaw. The Jewish Metropolis* (Leiden and Boston, 2015), 497-8.

nowhere else.[8]

Her work in the soup kitchen had convinced her that Jewish life in Warsaw was so deeply rooted and Jews were so numerous that its dominant role in Jewish cultural life would have continued for generations:

> ...despite everything we were surrounded by enormously powerful and dynamic Jewish folk masses, ...the Jewish masses were face to face with the spontaneous processes of emancipation and assimilation. But despite everything the masses were too numerous and too rooted in their culture for these processes to threaten the basic character of the nation. The religious strata...constituted an enormous reservoir of human resources and spiritual energy, and they were able to make up any losses we suffered [due to acculturation] – and even add to them.
>
> We thought we had arrived [in Jewish Warsaw] too late, after the best was already over. In fact, the blooms faded only to prepare for what would have been the next harvest of fruit, had it not been for the catastrophe that befell us.[9]

Before the war, she admitted, she had stressed the fading blossoms and the falling leaves, failing to see that these were a necessary prelude to a new second growth. Her goal was now to preserve the memory of this many-sided Jewish Warsaw.

At the same time, in her writings during the first years of the occupation and, indeed, after the mass deportation of the bulk of Warsaw Jewry, she was also filled with anger at the way the *Judenrat* and the Jewish Police had collaborated in the round-up of the Jews and at the failure of the Jews initially to resist the Nazi onslaught. When, on 26 July 1942 shortly after the beginning of the great deportation of Warsaw Jews to Treblinka, she handed over her first cache of writings to the *Oyneg Shabes* to be buried, she attached a note full of anger and despair:

> I am handing over this unfinished essay to the archive. The fifth day of the 'Aktion'. Perhaps such horrors have already occurred before in Jewish history. But such shame, never. Jews as tools [of the killers]. I want to stay alive. I am ready to kiss the boots of the worst scoundrel [*dem gemaynstn kham*] just to be able to see the moment of revenge,

8 For Auerbach's letter to Ravitch, see Natan Cohen, *Sefer, sofer veiton; hamercaz hatarbut hayehudit bevarsha* (Jerusalem, 2003), 257.
9 Varshever Tsavoes: *Bagegenishn, Aktivitetn, Goyroles, 1933–1945* (Tel Aviv, 1974), 22.

REVENGE REVENGE remember.[10]

These themes are well represented in 'Yizker 1943', written in November 1943 on the Aryan side after the Warsaw Ghetto uprising, in whose aftermath, the Nazis destroyed entirely what was left of the ghetto. This was a time of growing German terror against the Polish population. In a Warsaw tram she saw a Polish woman weeping over her son whom the Germans had just shot. She was struck by the fact that, concealing her identity as she was, she could not mourn in public, like the woman, whose lips moved like Hannah's in the Bible. It was now that she wrote, in Yiddish, rather than her usual Polish, her moving elegy.

> I may not groan and I may not cry.
>
> I may not call attention to myself on the street. And I have to cry so badly, have to groan. Not four times a year, but four times a day I want to say Yizker.

She poured out her soul as she tried to describe those who had perished – the toddlers, the children whom she remembered from the ghetto schools, the tough Jewish workers, the hardened women shopkeepers, young scouts, courting couples, intellectuals. This was the end of Jewish Warsaw.

She also described how the Germans had exploited the very qualities that had helped the Jews to survive in the Diaspora – their pragmatism, hard-headedness and natural optimism – to destroy them.

> And still other Jews – broad-shouldered, husky voiced, with rugged strength in their hearts and hands, artisans, workers. Teamsters and porters who could flatten any hooligan who dared invade their turf with a single blow of their fist.
>
> Where were you when they took your wives and children, your aged parents? What happened to make you run into the fire like oxen? Were you carried off by the flood with those who were weaker than you because there was no one to show you a way out of the panic?
>
> And you merchants from Nalewki Street, cunning, shrewd, in cut-off frock coats and caps, how did you fail to recognize the deadly fraud? Warsaw patriarchs and matriarchs, broad-beamed businesswomen among mountains of merchandise behind the cash-desks of their

10 Ringelblum Archive, Jewish Historical Institute; Part One, Document 655.

stores, big, strong faces glowing with wisdom over their three-fold double-chins.

> And you other mothers. Toil-weary market women – as disheveled and terrified as angry brood hens flapping their wings in fiery concern for their young.

She described what had happened as a flood:

> I saw a flood in the mountains once.
>
> Wooden cottages uprooted in the middle of the night bounced wildly on the furious river's waves, lamps still burning inside; men and women, children in cradles lashed to the rafters with ropes.
>
> Other huts, already empty, had tangles of hands growing out of their roofs. Fluttering like branches in a storm, desperately wringing, reaching vainly for help from the sky or the shore. Wide-open mouths could be seen from afar, but the roar of the waters drowned any screams.
>
> So did the Jewish masses flow to their deaths in the days of the deportation. They sank just as helplessly in the flood of utter destruction.

Given the elemental nature of the catastrophe, she clearly did not feel it appropriate to blame the Jewish masses for not resisting earlier.

Auerbach dealt with this question of resistance in *Der Yidisher Oyfshtand* written, like 'Yizker, in Yiddish, in Poland in the immediate post-war years in order to reach a Jewish audience. She was now concerned, above all, to commemorate Jewish heroism, linking the Uprising with the long trajectory of Jewish history. She pointed out that the Germans had decided to liquidate the ghetto during Passover. In this way

> ...they inadvertently helped to deepen an ancient symbol and make Passover a memorial to Jewish liberation all over again.
>
> Condemned to death, locked up in a walled-off ghetto, deprived of all their rights, isolated, debased, cut off from the world around them – in the face of certain annihilation, these Jews found the courage to launch an armed struggle against an enemy one hundred times stronger. The courage to embody the most urgent rights of the Jewish masses to

human and national life, their belief in the future of their people, their faith in the coming victory of freedom and justice – at the moment of their own death.

Passover Eve, 1943 – the date of the third and final murder-assault on the Jews of Warsaw. Also, the date of the Jewish revolt – the Jewish rising.

The Passover sacrifice would be burned alive this time.

Her goal in writing an account of the uprising was, in her words, to 'list the facts, one after the other, recite them in brief like a chronicle of our hearts, like a *megillah*, a scroll to be read anew every year'. At the end of the great deportation of June-September 1942, some 60-70,000 Jews remained in the ghetto, including some 35,000 slave labourers. Among them the mood was now increasingly militant. Certainly, until the destruction of the large majority of the community there had been many factors inhibiting the development of armed resistance. The view was widespread that some would survive and that resistance was suicidal and against Jewish interests. For the members of the Zionist youth movements, who were to play a key role in resistance, there was also the belief that European Jewry was doomed and that the future of Jewish life lay in Palestine. Fear was also an important factor in inhibiting resistance. In Auerbach's words, 'Anyone who wants to understand this fight has to understand terror. Active Jewish resistance cannot be understood by anyone who has not first understood the passive.' The all-pervasive hunger also undermined the desire for action, as did the awareness of the terrible consequences of revolt. The Germans certainly held the Jews collectively responsible for any actions against their rule. Political divisions among the Jews also hindered the growth of resistance. Zionists, Bundists (Jewish Socialists), Revisionists (Radical Zionists, followers of Zeev Jabotinsky and Menahem Begin) and Communists all had different ideas of how to resist. There was also the difficult problem of obtaining weapons.

Nevertheless, as Auerbach shows, Jews in Warsaw were now willing to resort to armed resistance under the impact of the humiliating effect of standing by and watching mass murder take place. When the great deportation in Warsaw ended on 12 September, those who favoured resistance met in a darkened room. According to one of them, Yitzhak Zuckerman, the meeting opened in an atmosphere of despair, the result of the fact that resistance had been impossible, because 'the masses did not believe us'. There were calls for an immediate and suicidal action:

In this atmosphere of despair it was impossible to say anything else.

So did the Jewish masses flow to their deaths in the days of the deportation

Nevertheless, one of the comrades plucked up his courage and said: the emotions are true; the conclusions are mistaken. The disaster is great, and so is the shame. But the deed that is being discussed here is a deed of despair. It will leave no echo. There will be no revenge on the enemy. Our youth will disappear. We have suffered an untold number of setbacks, and will yet suffer more. It is necessary to start from scratch...On that night we decided the fate of the January and April 1943 uprisings.[11]

There was also the moral aspect. Those present were clearly concerned with how they would be able to answer the question, 'What did all of you do when thousands and millions died?...Shall we answer that we looked for places to hide and let ourselves be led to death powerless just like the others?[12]

The establishment of a single unified underground in Warsaw had been delayed by the unwillingness of the Bund to join a common front with the Zionists, by the intransigence of the Revisionists and by an independent effort on the part of the communists to create an anti-fascist front in spring 1942, which collapsed when several of its leaders were arrested. Underground political activity with the goal of undertaking armed resistance had been discussed in the ghetto on 23 July 1942, the day after the beginning of the great deportation in the ghetto by the representatives of the major political parties. Arguing against resistance, Ignacy Schipper, the Zionist activist and historian, maintained that a proportion of the ghetto's inhabitants would survive if Nazi orders were complied with; violence would lead to certain annihilation. Arms were in short supply and there was no time to train fighters. When challenged subsequently by Mordechai Anielewicz, who was to be the leader of the Jewish Combatant Organization, he accused the young man of providing a strategy only for how best to die, whereas their aim should be to ensure the survival of a saving remnant.

Rabbi Zishe Fridman gave the view of the Orthodox *Agudas Yisrael:*

I believe in God and in miracles. God will not allow his people of Israel to be destroyed. We must long for the miracle and it will occur. Resistance is hopeless.[13]

Yet there were those who wanted to undertake armed resistance. On 28 July the Jewish Combatant Organization (*Żydowska Organizajca Bojowa* – ŻOB) was established and on 21 August, the first armed action had been taken in

11 Itzhak Zuckerman, 'Yemei September 1942", *Yalkut Moreshet*, no. 16, (1973), 32-3
12 This question was posed in Vilna in 1941 by Reizl Korczak. See Reizl Korczak, *Lehavot ba'efer* (Tel Aviv, 1965), 125..
13 See Hersh Berlinski, 'Zikhronot', in *Yalkut Moreshet* no. 16 (1963), 9-10.

the ghetto, an attempt on the life of the commander of the ghetto police, Jozef Szeryński, in which he was injured. Calls for military resistance intensified in the small ghetto left after the deportation of July – September and a complicated structure was now created which enabled the Bund and the Zionists to cooperate and create a large network of underground bunkers.

The Revisionists (the radical Zionists led first by Zeev Jabotinsky until his death in August 1940 and then by Menahem Begin) established their own organization, the Jewish Fighting Union (*Żydowski Związek Wojskowy* – ŻZW), which is alluded to in Auerbach's account but never directly discussed. The departure from Warsaw for Vilna in September 1939 of Menachem Begin, the leader of Betar (the youth movement of the Revisionist Zionists) in Poland from early 1939, weakened the movement significantly, as did his subsequent imprisonment by the Soviets, followed by his release and departure from the Soviet Union with the army established there by General Władysław Anders. Most of the leaders of the revisionist New Zionist Organization also left Warsaw and the movement was further demoralized by the death of its leader Vladimir ('Ze'ev') Jabotinsky in August 1940. It was only during the great deportation of Jews from the Warsaw Ghetto in the summer of 1942 that the ŻZW was established. It drew some of its support from members of Betar who had been working in an agricultural colony near Hrubieszów. Members of Betar were not represented at the meeting which set up the ŻOB and the ŻZW was only set up after it failed to be accepted into the ŻOB.

Both groups made contact with the Polish underground movements and obtained some weapons from them. It was clear that any revolt, given the enormous disparity of the forces involved would be suicidal, an assertion of Jewish dignity in the face of overwhelming Nazi power. Auerbach argues that with the war going badly, the Nazis were determined to liquidate the remaining ghettos, including that in Warsaw. When on 18 January 1943 they attempted to deport an additional 8,000 Jews from the Warsaw Ghetto, perhaps as a prelude to its total destruction, the ŻOB offered resistance. In a pamphlet issued on that day, it urged:

> Jews! The occupier is beginning the second act of our destruction. Do not go quietly to your deaths...Defend yourselves. Take an axe, a crowbar, a knife in your hands, barricade your homes, do not let them take you without resistance...In battle you have the hope of rescue...Fight.[14]

The Germans, astonished at the resistance they encountered, responded with

14 Quoted in Władysław Bartoszewski, 'The Martyrdom and Struggle of the Jews in Warsaw under German Occupation, 1939-1943', in Władysław T. Bartoszewski and Antony Polonsky (eds.) *The Jews in Warsaw: A History* (Oxford, 1991), 336.

a massive use of force. After several days, and the removal of between 5,000 and 6,500 people from the ghetto, they halted the deportation. They returned on 19 April, the eve of Passover, intending now to destroy the ghetto entirely. In response, 650 inadequately-armed young men and women, 500 from the Jewish Fighting Organization and around 150 from the Jewish Military Union, began the first major action of Jewish resistance against the Nazis.

On the fifth day of the insurrection the ŻOB issued an appeal, drafted by the Bundist, Ignacy Samsonowicz-Leszczyński drawing on the Polish and European insurrectionary tradition, which explained the decision to take up arms:

> Poles, Citizens, Soldiers of Freedom...
> Every doorstep in the ghetto has become a stronghold and will remain a stronghold until the end! All of us will probably perish in the fight, but we will never surrender!
> We, like you, burn with the desire to punish the enemy for his crimes, with the desire for vengeance. It is a fight for your freedom as well as for ours: for your human dignity as well as for ours!...[15]

The Uprising, which lasted more than three weeks, could not resist the German juggernaut. Auerbach fully documents its course and, in her detailed account, may have exaggerated its scope. The German commander, Jürgen Stroop, in his report claimed that 16 German troops were killed and 81 wounded. These figures may have been too low. They are never discussed by Auerbach. Certainly Stroop's goal was now finally to liquidate the ghetto and its inhabitants and the Jewish casualties were extremely high, as Auerbach demonstrates using Stroop's report. She does so with reluctance, observing that '[t]he enemy himself became the chronicler'. As the first major act of Jewish resistance to the Nazis, the Uprising certainly constituted an enormous fillip to the morale of Jews elsewhere wishing to resist. It also showed that the Jews, like the other national groups of the area, were capable of armed resistance.

Auerbach movingly describes the end of the uprising and the decision of the ŻOB leadership to commit collective suicide in the bunker from which they organized the fighting rather than allow themselves to be taken prisoner by the Germans. In her words:

> Mordechai Anielewicz, the commander of the revolt, died along with his army.
> Fate willed it so.

15 Ibid, 339-40.

> So that the very brightest of all lights might shine around the young hero's head.
>
> The halo of death.

Auerbach, who had many contacts on the 'Aryan' side, discusses the attitude of the non-Jewish Varsovians to the uprising in a nuanced way. After describing how German propaganda created among some of them hostility to the insurgents, she goes on:

> Taken aback by the protest against German crimes, by the horror of the murders and disgust with the miscreants among them, the best members of Polish society looked on at what was happening. Some left the city in terror. Others did what they could to help.
>
> The mood of the disinterested masses changed from one day to the next, from astonishment to approval of what the Jews were doing, to satisfaction at seeing the Germans hurt. Then doubt crept in, mixing poison into their pity. In the end they went back to their own affairs, their day-to-day concerns. The Philistines returned to their egoism and indifference.
>
> But the helpers did not give in. Not to fear, not to lies, not to hatred. Risked their lives to save a wretched Jewish child, Jewish strangers, close friends.
>
> Our brothers might have been lonely on the day of the final judgment, but they were not alone.

One of the most disputed questions about the Warsaw Ghetto uprising is the extent of assistance the Jewish resistance received from the Polish underground. This is discussed by Auerbach. In her view:

> The leaders of the Jewish Combat Organization had made every effort to win the support of the Polish underground movement for the Jewish preparations for the struggle.
>
> First, with respect to weapons.
> They turned to representatives of the government-in-exile and also sought to contact Polish military organizations.

In certain circles these Jewish efforts fell on deaf ears.

The Jewish Organization found full camaraderie and support only among *left-wing underground organizations* and their military formations.

Her assessment is confirmed by more recent research. The Home Army (*Armia Krajowa* – AK), the main Polish resistance movement from March 1943 linked with the Government-in-exile in London, was a large organization and contained within its ranks both those who were sympathetic to the plight of the Jews and those who retained their pre-war antisemitism. In his memoirs, written in the 1960s, Tadeusz Bor-Komorowski, its commander from March 1943, claimed he told the Jewish leadership in the ghetto that the organization was 'ready to come to the assistance of the Jews with supplies of arms and ammunition and to coordinate their attacks outside with Jewish resistance from within'. This offer, he claimed, was rejected because of the Jewish belief that 'if they behaved quietly the Germans might deport and murder 20,000 or 30,000 and perhaps even 60,000 of them, but it was inconceivable that they should destroy the lot; while if they resisted, the Germans would certainly do so'.[16]

There is no substance in these assertions. An AK officer, Henryk Woliński, was assigned at this time to be responsible for 'Jewish affairs', but his role was limited to gathering information. In fact the military underground provided no assistance to the Jews of Warsaw during the deportation and it was only on 17 September, when the deportation was practically over, that the *Związek Walki Czynnej* (the precursor of the Home Army) issued a statement condemning the German action. During this period, Arie Wilner ('Jurek'), who represented the Jewish Combatant Organization on the 'Aryan side', attempted to establish contact with the AK. As was noted later by Władysław Bartoszewski, 'he did indeed get through to cells in the AK, but ones that were not authorized to take decisions of this nature. Word of "Jurek's" mission did not reach the proper quarters in the AK Higher Command at the time.'[17] It was only after the deportation that he succeeded in establishing contact with Henryk Woliński, through the help of Alexander Kamiński, editor of *Biuletyn Informacyjny*, a link that was to be crucial in the transfer of such arms as were later obtained by the ŻOB from the AK.

At this stage, the Home Army High Command was determined to avoid a premature uprising now being called for by the communist People's Guard (*Gwardia Ludowa* – GL) and its successor from January 1944, the People's

16 Tadeusz Bor-Komorowski, *The Secret Army*, New York, 1951, 99-100.
17 Władysław Bartoszewski, Zofia Lewinówna, *Ten jest z ojczyznej mojej: Polacy z pomacą °ydom 1939-1945* (Kraków, 1969).

Army (*Armia Ludowa* – AL). During the deportation a clandestine paper of the GL's political superior, the Polish Workers' Party (PPR) had drawn the following lesson from the deportation of the Jews:

> Poles should realize that the rapid rate at which Hitler is being allowed to destroy the Jews will [only] speed up the murder of our people, the Poles. Thus the Jews who are actively resisting are also fighting for the lives of the Polish population, because they are causing the disorganization and debilitation of the abominable murder machine.[18]

Given the fear of a premature general revolt, General Stefan Rowecki, Commander of the AK, was unwilling to give the Jewish resistance significant quantities of arms. On 2 January 1943, he cabled London:

> Jews from all kinds of groups, including Communists, have turned to us lately asking for arms, as if we had depots full of them. As an experiment, I took out a few revolvers. I have no assurance that they will use these weapons at all. I shall not give out any more weapons, for you know that we ourselves have none. I am awaiting another shipment. Apprise me of what contact our Jews have with London.[19]

As Woliński was later to report, these supplies amounted to a total of ten revolvers.

Following the clashes in January 1943, the attitude of the military leadership softened and the contact established between Wilner and Woliński, as well as the links between the Bund and the Polish Socialists and between the Polish scouts and the pioneering groups in the ghetto, began to bear fruit. The new mood was described by Woliński in a report he prepared later:

> By order of the supreme commander, I held three consultations on this subject [the transfer of weapons] with the commander of 'Drapacz' [the code name for the Warsaw section of the AK] 'Konar' [General Chruściel, commander of this section]. He agreed to give the Warsaw Ghetto material aid and guidance and also mentioned the possibility of outside support from our units. They immediately set to work under

18 *Trybuna Chłopska* (6) August 1942.
19 Quoted in Yisrael Gutman, *The Jews of Warsaw, 1939–1945: Ghetto, Underground, Revolt* (Bloomington, Ind., 1982) 256. In the version published in Poland in the communist period, this was doctored to read 'Jews from all kinds of Communist groups.' On this issue, see Michał Borwicz, 'The Relations between the Polish and Jewish Underground', in *Jewish Resistance During the Holocaust, Proceedings of the Conference on Manifestations of Jewish Resistance* (Jerusalem, 1971), 348.

> the direction of 'Chirurg'. A link was set up between 'Jurek' and our officers. About fifty revolvers, a large quantity of ammunition, 80 kilos of explosive materials for the manufacture of 'bottles' [Molotov cocktails], and a certain quantity of grenades were turned over to the ŻOB. A workshop was put into operation in the ghetto to produce 'bottles.' In addition, the acquisition of arms, which the ŻOB engaged in on its own, was facilitated. A joint plan was formulated for fighting in the ghetto, and the support of our own units was anticipated.[20]

The quantity of arms was quite small and, in the case of the revolvers, not very effective in street fighting. Consequently, Mordechai Anielewicz, Commander of the ŻOB, wrote to the organization's representatives on the 'Aryan' side:

> ...Please inform the authorities in our name that if massive aid is not forthcoming immediately, we will view [their lack of action] as indifference...to the fate of the Jews of Warsaw. Allocating weapons without ammunition impresses [us] as a bitter mockery of our fate and confirms the assumption that the venom of antisemitism continues to permeate the ruling circles of Poland despite the tragic and brutal experience of the last three years...[21]

At this critical juncture, the developing cooperation was severely undermined by the arrest in March of Wilner, who had by now established his credentials with his Polish interlocutors. In addition, the fact that he was captured with weapons, against underground practice, revived fears about the professionalism of the Jewish underground. In the event, Wilner's actual position was not discovered by the Gestapo and he was replaced within six weeks by Yitshak Zuckerman. However the loss of momentum proved difficult to undo.[22]

The smaller Jewish Military Union (ŻZW), controlled by the Revisionist Zionists, who had some pre-war links with the Polish military and were impeccably anti-communist, had more initial success in obtaining weapons. This it achieved primarily through its contacts with the somewhat dubious character, Cezary Ketling-Szemley, who was operating on his own and buying and selling weapons on the black market. He does seem to have been able to sell the ŻZW a significant amount of weaponry. It also established links with Major Henryk Iwański ('Bystry'), an officer under the command of General

20 Woliński's report is reprinted in Ber Mark, *Powstanie w getcie warszawskim* (Warsaw, 1963), 342.
21 Quoted in Nachman Blumental and Joseph Kermish (ed.), *Hameri vehamered begeto Varsha*, Jerusalem, 1965, 125.
22 Mark, *Powstanie w getcie warszawskim*, 342.

Andrzej Petrykowski of the Security Corps (*Korpus Bezpieczeńtswa* – KB), an internal police force in the AK. It succeeded in building a tunnel to bring these arms into the ghetto and was able to acquire a few heavier weapons – submachine guns and a machine gun.

The main fighting conducted by the ŻZW was at Muranowska Square, where the organization had its headquarters. It now seems probable that during this fighting the ŻZW hoisted two flags, the white and red Polish flag and the blue and white Zionist flag, something discussed by Auerbach. She was not sure whether this had occurred, observing:

> Blue and white, white and red, waving side by side.
>
> A call to arms to the Jews, a battlefield greeting to the Poles.
>
> True or not, it's a beautiful story.
>
> A legend was starting to take shape in the mouths of the common people, a popular legend about the revolt of the Jews.

After three days of heroic fighting in Muranowska Square, in which one of its leader, Leon Rodal seems to have lost his life, the survivors withdrew to the 'Aryan' side where they were betrayed and liquidated first in Michalin, a village near Warsaw, and subsequently on Grzybowski Square, where another of its leaders, Paweł Frenkel seems to have been killed in mid-June 1943.

The outbreak of the revolt in April caught the AK Command by surprise. As late as 10 April 1943, General Rowecki in a cable to London spoke of the impending liquidation of the ghetto but gave no indication that he expected armed resistance.[23] For the *Armia Krajowa* Command, the fear that the communists could exploit the uprising in order to provoke a 'premature' uprising remained strong. It is certainly true that the ŻOB had established good relations with the Polish Workers's Party (PPR) and that it did not share the anti-communism of the AK. The *Gwardia Ludowa* was certainly sympathetic to the ŻOB's goal of preparing an uprising, since it hoped this would spark off further Polish resistance, something which is recognized by Auerbach.[24]

One way that the AK attempted to contain the influence of the communists was by the evacuation of the fighting members of the ŻOB so that they could participate in guerilla activities elsewhere. The *Armia Krajowa* Command appears to have been thinking of Volhynia, which was wracked by a brutal

23 Ibid., document 40, 226.
24 Gutman, *The Jews of Warsaw*, 301.

‘Prepare to defend yourselves!’Members of the Hashomer Hatzair socialist Zionist youth movement. Back row, left to right: Tzvi Braun, Shifra Sokolka and Mordechai Anielewicz. Seated in front are Moshe Domb and Rachel Zilberberg (‘Sarenka’)

Members of the Hashomer Hatzair, left to right: Aron Szwarc, Tamar (last name unknown), Lodzia Hamersztajn, and Berel Lemel

ethnic conflict between Poles and Ukrainians and where the AK was eager to cooperate with Jewish partisans to defend Polish villages.[25] A day or two before the actual outbreak of the revolt, Woliński told Zuckerman that 'we are being asked not to rebel in the ghetto but to go out to the forests.' When Zuckerman expressed the ŻOB's determination to fight in Warsaw, he replied 'The command has decided that it is premature to fight in Warsaw...They are willing to do everything necessary to prepare combat bases for us in the forests.'[26]

Zuckerman has also described a meeting with a senior AK officer 'who introduced himself as Grenadier Karol'. In response to a request for arms, Karol responded by suggesting the removal of fighters from the ghetto. Zuckerman responded: 'The combat companies will not leave the ghetto as long as they have a single bullet left in [their] rifles to shoot themselves with.' Zuckerman subsequently demanded 'that automobiles and people be prepared in time to get the survivors out; that houses [be readied] to take in and conceal the fighters.' Karol replied:

> Actually, I can speak to you frankly: We don't believe you. We believe that the ghetto is no more than a base for Soviet Russia. A plan exists, and [we] Poles know what it is. The Russians are the ones who have prepared the revolt in the Warsaw Ghetto, and you have far more weapons than you let on; and I am sure that on 1 May 1943, they will land parachutists in the Warsaw Ghetto.

Karol continued:

> There is anxiety among the Polish public that the revolt will spread beyond the ghetto and the Poles will rise up [in rebellion], which is what the [PPR] wants. So I warn you: If this comes to pass, and if you collaborate with the GL and it comes to your aid, we will move against the ghetto!'[27]

The view that the communists were a key element in the Uprising and that it was intended to serve communist goals was also to be found in the AK's intelligence service. One report on fighting in the ghetto had information that:

> German intelligence had received a tip on 20 April 1943 that a Communist organized uprising would break out within the borders of

25 Blumental and Kermish, *Hameri vehamered begeto Varsha*, 399.
26 Quoted in Gutman, *The Jews of Warsaw*, 418.
27 Ibid.

> the General Gouvernement. Since the headquarters of Communist activity was in the ghetto, it was decided to put a stop to these activities by [taking] counteraction... According to a rumour, the Jewish insurgents were led by a Pole, Dr. Adolf Kohn, and a sergeant who had deserted from the German army. The number of Jews who took part in the military action is not known. [Yet] according to the rumour, units of the Polish Communists are fighting alongside the Jews...[28]

It was claims such as these that led the Polish Minister of Defence, General Marian Kukiel, to cable the commander of the armed forces in the underground to query:

> Was the resistance of the Jews of Warsaw during the liquidation of the ghetto really led and organized by Soviet officers and noncommissioned officers parachuted into the ghetto, and were arms, ammunition, and antitank guns supplied in the same fashion? [29]

In the first days of the Uprising both the AK and the GL mounted operations in solidarity with the ghetto fighters. They were on a relatively small scale and the later claim by General Chruściel that he was instructed by General Bor-Komorowski, who had taken over as Commander of the *Armia Krajowa* after General Rowecki's capture by the Germans in March 1943, to draw up a comprehensive plan to assist the ghetto is lacking in substance. According to General Chruściel:

> The plan was simple: to breach the ghetto walls and facilitate the escape of those who were able to flee. Toward this end we intended to breach [the wall] at a number of places on the Parysowska and Stawki side to permit movement in the direction of Kampinos Forest. To divert the Germans [we would] attack them first along the entire circumference of the ghetto wall. Those unable to march on foot...would be taken out through the sewers.[30]

The existence of such a plan seems unlikely. It would have required close cooperation with the ŻOB, of which there is no record, while the actions undertaken by the *Armia Krajowa* during the uprising were on a much more limited scale. In addition there does not seem to have been any preparation

28 Mark, *Powstanie w getcie warszawskim*, document 76, 290-1.
29 Cable from General Kukiel in Polish Underground Study Trust, quoted in Gutman, *The Jews in Warsaw*, 410-11.
30 Blumental and Kermish, *Hameri vehamered begeto Varsha*, document 148, 406-8.

to accommodate Jewish fighters on the 'Aryan' side.

The second day of the uprising did witness two abortive 'support actions' by the Polish underground, one carried out by the *Armia Krajowa* and the other by the *Gwardia Ludowa*. In the first, a band of fighters from the AK under the command of Major Józef Pszenny ('Chwacki'), attempted to break through the wall on Bonifraterska Street. The Polish unit moved up the wall at six in the evening. One mine was detonated but it failed to breach the wall and the Polish Police observing the activity called in the Germans. Two AK fighters (Jozef Wilk and Eugeniusz Morawski) were killed and two others were wounded in this clash.

In the second, a combat group of the *Gwardia Ludowa*, under the command of Franciszek Bartoszek ('Jacek') and including the Jewish fighter Niuta Tejtelbaum, attacked a German artillery crew stationed on Nowiniarska Street. The action began at about seven in the evening. According to the Polish version of events, the German crew (made up of two men) was hit and silenced, while another GL group (under the command of Jerzy Lerner – 'Mietek') attempted to attack the German sentries at the corner of Gęsia and Okopowa Streets. This latter attack failed because before the unit could approach the Germans, it encountered a group of Polish hooligans who ganged up on its Jewish commander. The scuffle with the Poles roused the attention of the German force and the Polish unit dispersed. Lerner was killed by German gunfire. During the first days of the revolt, the PPR also gave the ŻOB twenty five rifles, but they could not be transferred to the ghetto and were not employed in the fighting.

Polish military formations did play some role in the escape of fighters from the ghetto. As Auerbach points out:

> It had been agreed that when further combat became impossible, they would organize the withdrawal of their remaining forces from the ghetto. The survivors were to be taken out and sent to the partisans in the forests, where they could continue the struggle against the common enemy.

The ŻZW fighters who left the ghetto early in the fighting were assisted by their connections in the KB, the Security Corps of the AK. In the actions to rescue ŻOB fighters a significant role was played by the *Gwardia Ludowa*. The role of the *Armia Krajowa* in this action, was, as Yisrael Gutman has argued, not 'significant'.[31]

One unit of the ŻOB under Yitshak Zuckerman, which had remained in

31 Blumental and Kermish, *Hameri vehamered begeto Varsha*, document 148 425.

Warsaw, took part in the Warsaw uprising of August-September 1944, organized by the *Armia Krajowa* at a time when German power, in the aftermath of the attempt in July on Hitler's life, appeared to be collapsing. The goal was to create an authority linked with the Polish government in London with which the Soviets, now moving westward and about to occupy Poland, would have to cooperate. As is well known, this strategy failed tragically. During the Uprising, an AK unit freed Jewish prisoners from the Gęsiówka concentration camp, created to salvage valuables from the ruins of the ghetto. Many of them also participated in the uprising. At the same time the National Armed Forces (*Narodowe Sily Zbrojne*), and some units of the AK, in particular the 'Hala' battalion of Captain Wacław Stykowski, were responsible for the murder of scores of Jews who now emerged from their hideouts.[32]

Mordechai Anielewicz left a final letter, written on 23 April, four days after the beginning of the Uprising, to Yitshak Zuckerman on the 'Aryan' side, which expresses the way the ŻOB understood the uprising, He wrote:

> I am unable to describe to you the conditions in which the Jews are currently forced to live. Only a few individuals will endure it; sooner or later, the rest will die...Be well, my friend. Perhaps we will see one another again. The most important thing is that my life's dream has come true. Jewish self-defence in the ghetto has been realized. Jewish retaliation and resistance has become a fact. I have been witness to the heroic battle of the Jewish fighters.[33]

Auerbach concludes her account by memorializing these fighters (see page 200). She does so, as was done on the Umschlagplatz memorial, located on the place from which most Warsaw Jews were deported to Treblinka, by listing their first names, providing in this way both a moving memorial and a clear example of her goals in writing *Der Yidisher Oyfshtand.*

32 Michał Cichy, 'PolacyŻydzi: Czarne Karty Powstania Warszawskiego', *Gazeta Wyborcza*, 29/30 January 1994. See also *Intelligence Report: Article on Warsaw Uprising Touches Raw Nerve in Polish-Jewish Relations No. 8*, April 1994, published by the Institute of Jewish Affairs, (London, 1994); and Gabriel Finder, 'Jewish Prisoner Labour in Warsaw after the Ghetto Uprising', *Polin,* volume 17, 325-52.

33 Yitzhak Arad, Yisrael Gutman and A. Margoliot (eds.) *Documents on the Holocaust: Selected Sources on the Destruction of the Jews of Germany and Austria, Poland and the Soviet Union* (Jerusalem, 1987), document 145.

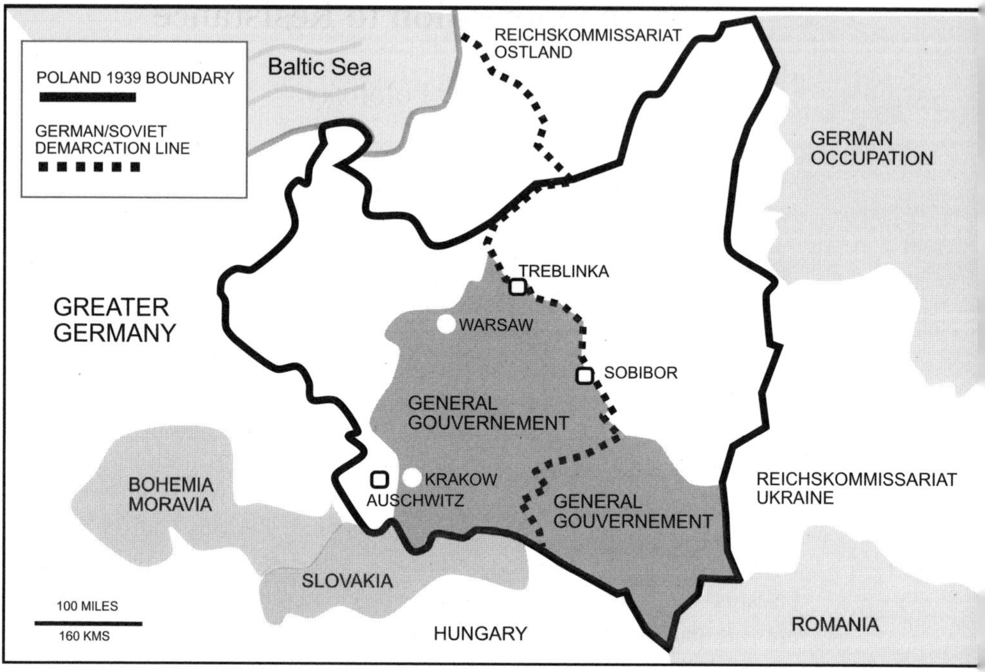

Poland: October 1939 to June 1941:
territories annexed by Germany and the Soviet Union

The Warsaw Ghetto – From Oppression to Resistance

Antony Polonsky

> Let the earth not cover my blood and let my cry find no rest.
>
> Job

> Nowadays, death rules in all its majesty; while life hardly glows under a thick layer of ashes. Even this faint glow of life is feeble, miserable and weak, poor, devoid of any spiritual content. The very soul, both in the individual and in the community, seems to have starved and perished, to have dulled and atrophied. There remains only the needs of the body – and it leads merely an organic-physiological existence.
>
> Yet we wish to live on, to continue our existence as free and creative men. This shall be our test. If, under the thick layer of ashes, our life is not extinguished, this will prove the triumph of the human over the inhuman – that our will to live is mightier than the will to destruction, that we are capable of overcoming all the evil forces which are attempting to engulf us.
>
> Abraham Lewin, *A Cup of Tears. A Diary of the Warsaw Ghetto*

The Nazi invasion of Poland on 1 September 1939 followed by the country's rapid defeat and its partition by Germany and the Soviet Union under the terms of the German-Soviet Non-Agresssion Agreement was an important step forward in Hitler's plans to establish a German Empire in Europe. It also contributed significantly to the waging of what Lucy Dawidowicz has rightly characterized as his 'war against the Jews'. To Hitler and his closest adherents, the fiction of a Jewish conspiracy to destroy the German people provided a central motif which could unite the disparate elements making up Nazi doctrine. Though the new Germany had been relatively slow to put into practice the more extreme aspects of Nazi antisemitism, by 1938 the regime was set in its deep-seated hatred of the Jews and its determination to root out

Attention Germans! The Jewish owners of Shops 5PS are the destroyers and gravediggers of German production. They pay slave wages to German workers. The chief owner is Natan Shmidt

Jewish influence wherever this could be achieved. That year had seen the unleashing in November of a ferocious campaign of anti-Jewish violence, generally known as the *Kristallnacht*, in response to the assassination in Paris of a German diplomat by a desperate Jewish youth. In the Reichstag on 30 January 1939, Hitler threatened:

> If the international Jewish money power in Europe and beyond succeeds in enmeshing the peoples in a world war, the result will not be the Bolshevization of the world and a victory for Jewry, but the annihilation of the Jewish race in Europe.[1]

In those parts of Poland which the Nazis occupied after the Polish defeat, the new regime did not immediately implement these threats of genocide. However, in sporadic anti-Jewish violence during and after the September campaign about 5,000 Jews lost their lives at Nazi hands. Many synagogues and Jewish libraries were burnt, most notably the famous library of the Khakhmey Lublin Yeshiva.

Nazi policy for the Jews in occupied Poland was laid down as early as 21 September 1939 by Reinhard Heydrich, head of the Reich Main Security Office. According to his directives, Jews were to be expelled from the area to be directly incorporated into the Third Reich and sent into the General Gouvernement, which was to comprise the remainder of Poland annexed by the Nazis and which was to be ruled as a colonial territory in which Polish national aspirations would be brutally suppressed. In order to control the Jews more easily, they were to be concentrated in ghettos, which were to be closed off from the surrounding population. These were to be administered by Jewish councils (*Judenräte*), which would be 'fully responsible in the literal sense of the word for the exact and punctual execution of all directives issued or yet to be issued.'[2] At this stage, the Nazis had not yet adopted a goal of mass-murder of the Jews. Rather, their aim was to impoverish and plunder them, exploiting their labour. They were still prepared to consider the possibility of emigration, which was only stopped in practice from the General Gouvernement in the summer of 1940 and prohibited from the Third Reich in November 1941. Jewish conditions were deliberately kept as harsh as possible. By 1941, for instance, the daily food ration for a Jew in Warsaw was 184 calories, compared to 669 for a Pole and 2,613 for a German.[3] The hope was in this way to starve

1 Quoted in N. Baynes (ed.), *The Speeches of Adolf Hitler*, vol. 1, April 1922-August 1939 (London, 1942), 741.
2 For this, see M. Broszat, *Nationalsozialistische Polenpolitik 1939-1945*, revised edn. (Munich, 1963), 20-2.
3 E. Duraczyński, *Wojna i Okupacja* (War and Occupation) (Warsaw, 1974), p. 69. II Diary entry for 19 Dec. 1939, S. Piotrowski (ed.), *Hans Frank's Diary* (Warsaw, 1961).

a significant proportion of the Jewish population.

The Nazis initially hesitated to close off the sections of Warsaw in which they had compelled all the Jews of the Polish capital to concentrate. However, a further stage in the persecution of the Jews came on 16 November 1940, when, in an action unprecedented in recent European history, they sealed this area and forbade Jews to leave it. It included districts with a substantial Jewish population, but in order to ensure that all Jews in Warsaw resided in this area and that non-Jews were excluded, the occupiers forced 113,000 Poles and 138,000 Jews to change their dwelling places. In this way was established what has come to be known as the Warsaw 'ghetto'. This was not a term to the liking of the Nazis. They forbade its use in the government-controlled Polish and Jewish press in occupied Poland, insisting that the area be referred to rather as the Jewish Residential District (*Wohnbezirk).*

Nearly 450,000 people were confined in a small number of city blocks. Overcrowding was appalling. According to a post-war estimate, the population density was 128,000 per square km. and the number of people forced to live in each room was more than nine. The area was, in fact, neither a 'Jewish residential district' nor a 'ghetto' but a combination of the largest Jewish 'prison city' in Europe and a forced labour camp.

The establishment of the ghetto in Warsaw closed off from the rest of the city and the transfer of a quarter of a million people which it entailed was accompanied by heart-rending scenes of terrible hardship. In the words of an eye-witness, Toshia Bialer:

> Try to picture one-third of a large city's population moving through the streets in an endless stream, pushing wheeling, dragging all their belongings from every part of the city to one small section, crowding one another more and more as they converged. No cars, no horses, no help of any sort were available to us by order of the occupying authorities. Pushcarts were about the only method of conveyance we had, and these were piled high with household goods, furnishing much amusement to the German onlookers who delighted in overturning the carts and seeing us scrambling for our effects. Many of the goods were confiscated arbitrarily without any explanation.
>
> In the ghetto, as some of us had begun to call it, half-ironically and in jest, there was appalling chaos. Thousands of people were rushing around at the last minute trying to find a place to stay. Everything was already filled up, but still they kept on coming and somehow room was found. The narrow, crooked streets of the most dilapidated parts of Warsaw

> were crowded with pushcarts, their owners going from house to house asking the inevitable question: Have you room? The sidewalks were covered with their belongings. Children wandered, lost and crying, parents ran hither and yon seeking them, their cries drowned in the tremendous hubbub of half a million uprooted people.[4]

The first fifteenth months of the ghetto's existence was a period when the Nazis were still undecided about how they would 'solve' the 'Jewish problem'. Indeed, most Jews remained convinced that they would be able to survive German persecution until the Allied victory in which they fervently believed. During this period, the ghetto and its institutions seemed to achieve a modicum of stability. The *Judenrat*, headed by the assimilated engineer Adam Czerniaków hoped by the sedulous implementation of the Germans' directives to protect the Jews from the worst consequences of Nazi rule until the dawn of better times. The powers of the *Judenrat* were considerably larger than those of the Warsaw *kehilla*[5] from which it claimed to be derived. Yet its role was, above all, to carry out the orders given by the Nazi authorities to the ghetto. It was, in addition, responsible for distributing food, accommodation and work as well as organizing public services. It was authorized to impose taxes to pay for its activities.

The role of mediator between the German authorities and the inhabitants of the ghetto was a thankless one and the *Judenrat* was soon the target of bitter attacks from those it was trying to serve. Indeed, the Germans well understood that by using the council to impose their will on the ghetto, they could deflect much Jewish hostility away from themselves.

Many of the leading members of the *Judenrat* had previously held positions in the Jewish community and clearly regarded themselves as charged with a special responsibility made all the heavier by the flight from Warsaw (along with many members of the Polish elite) of many Jewish leaders. Czerniaków's diary shows him to have been a somewhat unimaginative if benevolent individual, with little faith in the abilities of the average individual inhabitant of the ghetto, but it also shows his motives in assuming and exercising office to have been above reproach. He was well aware of his powerlessness. As he wrote in his diary, 'I have to suffer in a stuffy room which looks like a prison cell... Besides all these Jewish complaints.'[6] His sense of responsibility was also shared by a number of the other leading members of

4 T. Bialer, 'Recollections', *Colliers*, New York, 20 Feb. 1943, 17, quoted in Martin Gilbert, *The Holocaust: The Jewish Tragedy* (London, 1986), 129-30.
5 The elected council which governed the Jewish community.
6 *The Warsaw Diary of Adam Czerniakow: Prelude to Doom*, ed. Raul Hilberg, Stanislaw Staron and Josef Kermish (New York, 1979), 172.

the *Judenrat* such as Abraham Gepner, who before the war had been chairman of the Union of Jewish Merchants and a member of the Warsaw City Council, Shmuel Winter, who had been active in YIVO, (the Jewish Scientific Organization), a scholarly body established in Wilno in 1925 and who had many links in the ghetto with the underground opposition and Jozef Jaszuński, who had been head of ORT, the Jewish vocational training organization in Poland.

The *Judenrat* quickly developed a large civil service to carry out its functions. Whereas the pre-war Kehilla had employed barely 530 persons, the *Judenrat* staff soon grew to over 6,000, including special departments for Economic Affairs, the Budget, Labour, Health, Social Welfare and Burial. It organized a large vocational training network, sometimes without the knowledge of the German authorities. When in October 1941 the Germans gave official permission for the reopening of schools, it set up a school network based on the various ideological groupings (Zionist, Bundist [Jewish Socialist] and Religious) into which the pre-war private Jewish school system had been divided. This provided school places for 7,000 of the 50,000 children in the ghetto.

Even before this date, education had been carried on clandestinely. This was one of the principal ways the inhabitants of the ghetto sought to counteract the Nazi attempt to reduce them to sub-humans. We have a number of descriptions of Jewish education in the ghetto. According to Nehama Eckheizer Fahn, who attended the Yehudia Girls' School at this time:

> I was destined to be at Yehudia during World War II. Almost the entire staff, with Stefania Schweiger at their head, continued to teach...
>
> Lessons were conducted in a different place every day, in the houses of teachers or pupils. They were conducted clandestinely in small groups, by the light of a single candle, each evening somewhere else. More than once teachers or staff were ill or weak from hunger, but I don't think there was ever more enthusiastic studying or teaching. It was not an escape from the dreadful reality but an expression of opposition to the iniquity and the desecration of cherished values. Over and over again, the teachers emphasized that even in times such as these we must not abandon human values. They hoped that their pupils would stay alive and tried to maintain their spiritual integrity. Relationships between teachers and pupils also changed – continual fear in the cold evenings in darkened rooms created strong ties and great affection between us. We became one family. I remember particularly the last full assembly

> of the school, which took place in an institute for abandoned children. We sang and we danced, even though the tension in the ghetto had reached its height and we knew that the end was very near. At the end of the party one of the teachers got up and said: 'If we stay alive after this war, we shall try to live as human beings worthy of that exalted title; and if it has been decreed that we are to die – we shall die proudly. Whatever our fate is to be, there is no doubt in my heart that the world that emerges after this war will be a better place.'[7]

The *Judenrat* was also responsible for the establishment and administration of a Supply Authority (*Zakład Zaopatrzenia*) which distributed ration cards and was responsible for the provision of the small amount of food which the ghetto authorities were legally allowed to purchase as well as for the obtaining of other essential goods, above all coal. It even undertook from the beginning of 1941 to organize a postal service in the ghetto. According to its contract with the Post Office administration in Warsaw, the workers in this Jewish Post, with its headquarters at 19 Zamenhof Street, were to receive all post addressed to the Jewish population in bulk. This included not only letters but also food parcels both from occupied Poland and from neutral countries, of which, until June 1941 the most important was the Soviet Union.[8]

The essential fact, however, given the nature of German policy, was that the *Judenrat* was in an impossible situation. Its position was further undermined by the presence within it of many opportunists and people prepared to profit from the situation, not to speak of outright German agents. In addition, some of its policies reflected its socially conservative outlook and its willingness to sacrifice those it regarded as expendable in the interests of the higher good of ensuring the survival of at least some of those in the ghetto. Thus, for instance, its policy of using indirect taxation to finance its needs bore heavily on the poorest elements in the ghetto. Similarly, when required to supply men for forced labour, the *Judenrat* tended to take those who had least influence or position. These policies were maintained in spite of the establishment of public watchdog committees on which sat prominent social activists such as Ignacy Schipper and Shakhne Sagan, who were attached to agencies of the Judenrat, with the task of monitoring their activities.

In order to maintain order, the Nazis instructed the *Judenrat* to establish a *Jüdischer Ordnungsdienst* (Jewish Service for the Maintenance of Order)

7 Quoted in the Hebrew edition of Abraham Lewin's diary, Mipinkaso shel hamoreh mi-Yehudia: Geto Varshe, April 1942-Januar 1943 (ed. Tsvi Shner, Beit Lohamei Hagetaot, 1969), 12-13.
8 On the postal service, see R. Sakowska, 'Łączność pocztowa warszawskiego getta', Biuletyn Żydowskiego Instytutu Historycznego, 45-6, 94-109 and Y. Gutman, The Jews of Warsaw, 1939-1943. Ghetto, Underground, Revolt (Brighton, 1982), 111.

which became known as the Jewish police or ghetto police. Headed by Józef Szeryński, a Jewish convert to Catholicism who before the war had been a colonel in the Polish police, it was first organized on a voluntary basis and numbered initially about 1,000 members. Its enrolment rose by December 1941 to about 1,600 and to nearly 2,200 in July 1942 on the eve of the great deportation from the ghetto to the Treblinka death camp. Within its ranks it contained a considerable number of educated people, above all men who had been officers in the Polish army as well as many lawyers. Since it did not possess the power to deal with crimes, it was obliged in the case of such offences to hand suspects over to the pre-war Polish police, the so-called *Policja granatowa* (navy-blue police, from the colour of its uniforms), which the Nazis kept in being. In practice, there was a marked disinclination to resort to such drastic action and the Jewish police often acted as arbitrators in criminal disputes, meting out a rough-and-ready but usually accepted justice. Ultimately, the ghetto police were responsible to the German authorities, above all the *Sicherheitsdienst* (Secret Service) and Gestapo, by whom it was strictly controlled.

Initially ghetto opinion was not unsympathetic to the Jewish police. Mary Berg recorded in her diary: 'I experience a strange and utterly illogical feeling of satisfaction when I see a Jewish policeman at a crossing – such policemen were entirely unknown in pre-war Poland.'[9] Similarly Chaim Kaplan, who was usually very harsh in his judgments, wrote on 21 December 1940:

> The residents of the ghetto are beginning to think they are in Tel Aviv. Strong bona fide policemen from among our brothers, to whom you can speak in Yiddish! First of all it comes as a godsend to the street vendors. The fear of the Gentile police is gone from their faces. A Jewish policeman, a man of human sensibilities – one of our brothers – would not turn over their baskets or trample their wares. The other citizens of the ghetto are relieved, too, because a Jewish shout is not the same as a Gentile one. The latter is coarse, crude, nasty; the former, while it may be threatening, contains a certain gentility, as if to say: 'Don't you understand?'[10]

Yet even before the great deportation of July-September 1942, in which the Jewish police made itself notorious by its cooperation with the Nazis in rounding up Jews, the police had become a hated symbol of authority.

Although initially German policy had been concerned ruthlessly to exploit

9 *The Diary of Mary Berg*, ed. SL Schneiderman (New York, 1945), entry for 22 December 1940.
10 *The Warsaw Diary of Chaim A. Kaplan*, translated and edited by Abraham Katsch (New York, 1973), 234. This is the English version of *Yoman Geto Varshe* (Tel Aviv, 1966).

Jewish labour while at the same time expropriating Jewish industry, the occupying authorities gradually came to the realization that they might be able to benefit from Jewish economic skills. This conflict between those who wished to profit from the exploitation of the Jews and those who favoured their destruction was to continue throughout the war. The *Judenrat* was eager to respond to the new German mood, believing that if the Jews made themselves indispensable to the German war effort, they would have a better chance to survive. This was a widespread view in the ghetto. Ringelblum recorded in his diary in March 1942 that 'within the community, there are those who claim that the danger of deportation which hangs over us has now passed thanks to the workshops that are producing for the German army.'[11] The *Judenrat* tried to expand employment by attracting German-owned or supervised plants to the ghetto. In August 1941, it even sanctioned the establishment of an incorporated company which was to foster crafts, the ghetto authorities providing orders, finance and tools. In addition, many Jews were employed in semi-legal workshops, which supplied not only the Polish black market but even the German authorities and the Wehrmacht.

The number of people involved in these activities has been variously estimated. In July 1942, the Labour Department of the Judenrat, which was directly supervised by the Germans, assessed the number of workers in the ghetto as 70,000 (60,000 men and 10,000 women). This, of course, meant that there was a very large group (according to some estimates numbering, with dependents, as many as 200,000) which had no means, apart from the sale of their property and their savings of providing a livelihood for themselves. In these circumstances, widespread poverty was a feature of ghetto life. According to the post-war memoirs of Stefan Ernest, a senior *Judenrat* official:

> Perhaps twenty, perhaps thirty thousand properly nourished people, are members of the 'social elite'. In contrast are the masses of a quarter of a million beggars and totally destitute, who struggle just to postpone the hour of death from starvation... And in the middle, between these two ends of the spectrum, a mass of about 200,000 'average people' who make do, more or less, and are still considered 'personalities', still surviving decently dressed, their bodies not swollen by hunger.[12]

Poverty inevitably gave rise to malnutrition. We have already seen how low

11 Emanuel Ringelblum, *Ksovim fun geto* vol. I: 1939-42, vol. II 1942-3, (eds.) Artur Eisenbach, T. Berenstein, Ber Mark, Adam Rutkowski (Warsaw, 1961, 1963), vol. 1, 348. On the economic situation in the ghetto see Gutman, *The Jews of Warsaw*, 72-7, and Kermish, *To Live with Honor and Die with Honor*, 533-84.
12 Stefan Ernest, 'Diary', 74-5. In Yad Vashem archives, 0-6/103.

Jewish rations were (184 calories per day), far below what was needed for survival. One consequence was the very high death rate in the ghetto, the result both of starvation and the susceptibility to disease induced by malnutrition. Between January 1941 and July 1942 nearly 61,000 people died in the ghetto mostly from these causes. Hunger was one of the factors which made political organization and resistance much more difficult.

The diarist Abraham Lewin described the poverty and hunger which characterized ghetto life as follows:

> We live in a prison. We have been degraded to the level of homeless and uncared-for animals. When we look at the swollen, half-naked bodies of Jews lying in the streets, we feel as if we found ourselves at some subhuman level. The half-dead, skeletal faces of Jews, especially those of dying little children, frighten us and recall pictures of India, or of the isolation-colonies for lepers which we used to see in films. Reality surpasses any fantasy; and possibly one thing could still surprise us is would be mass murder in the place of the systematic extermination.[13]

Hunger and the widespread shortage of food gave rise to extensive smuggling.

Even before the establishment of the ghetto, the introduction by the Germans of strict rationing as well as control over what farmers produced had created severe problems over food supply for both Poles and Jews in the towns. Under these conditions, food smuggling became widespread. The creation of the ghetto did not stop this illicit trade in food – on the contrary, given the desperate shortage of food there, it encouraged its further development.

The attitude of the German authorities towards smuggling was not wholly consistent. In principle, it was strongly opposed and often ruthlessly repressed. At the same time many within the administration, from the highest to the lowest echelons, were prepared to tolerate a degree of illicit trading in food, partly because of its lucrative by-products in the form of bribes and confiscations and partly because it alleviated somewhat the famine conditions in the ghetto and thus kept the ghetto work-force in better condition. Similarly, smuggling was only possible because of the complaisance of many members of both the Polish and Jewish police, both of which were ultimately dependent on the occupying authorities.

Smuggling was undertaken partly by individuals who hoped, in this way,

13 'Eulogy Read at a Commemorative Evening in Honour of Yitshak Meir Weissenberg, 13 September 1941', reproduced in Abraham Lewin, *A Cup of Tears. A Diary of the Warsaw Ghetto* (Oxford, 1988), 243.

to provide for themselves and their families. Many of them were people who worked on the Aryan side. Children too, were frequently engaged in the clandestine transfer of food. It was also carried out in a more organized way by professional smugglers who, in fact, provided most of the food consumed in the ghetto. It was a profitable if risky operation and many of those who became active in it paid with their lives. According to the study of smuggling, written in the ghetto by Mojzesz Passenstein for the underground archive organized by the *Oyneg Shabes* group:

> The lives of the smugglers were filled with danger. Not a day passed when one of them was not cut down by machine-gun fire from the gendarmes, but the smuggling did not stop. After the corpse was removed, it continued with the same intensity and the same temptation of the fates which placed the smugglers at the front line of the ghetto's struggle against Hitlerism.[14]

Many of the smugglers were people who before the war had performed tough labouring occupations like portering. Some were simply members of Warsaw's Jewish underworld. They became part of the new ghetto elite, able to enjoy a relatively high standard of living on the proceeds of their operation. Yet they were generally respected. In the conclusion of his study of smuggling in the ghetto, Passensein observes that 'the role of the smugglers in the struggle against the evil plan of the authorities to starve the Jewish population was so great that they deserve to be placed in the first rank of those who fought the tyrant.'[15] Henryka Lazowert's poem in Polish, 'The Little Smuggler' was widely read at gatherings in the ghetto. Ringelblum described it as 'a song in praise of the thousands of children who endangered themselves countless numbers of times in order to sustain their families and the community as a whole.' Its last verse reads:

> I shall not return to you again
> No more a voice from afar,
> The dust of the street is my grave
> An infant's fate is sealed
> And on my lips alone
> A single care is frozen

14 Mojżesz Passenstein, 'Smugiel w getcie warszawskim', *Biuletyn* Żydowskiego Instytutu Historycznego, 26, 69.
15 Ibid., 71.

Who, dear Mother,
Will bring you a crust tomorrow?[16]

Rachel Auerbach, in her book *Behutstot Varshe* (*In the Streets of Warsaw 1939-1943*, in Hebrew, Tel Aviv, 1954), accords 'a place of honour to Jewish and Polish smugglers alike...for their persistence and bravery in the on-going battle between unequal parties...honour to the unknown smuggler, the grey soldier on the walls of the besieged city.'[17] Similarly, Leon Berensohn, the renowned Polish-Jewish lawyer and veteran defendant in political trials, advocated after the end of the war the erection of a monument to the 'unknown smuggler'.[18]

There was one organization in the ghetto which while loosely linked with the *Judenrat* retained a degree of both integrity and independence. This was the Jewish Self-help Organization, which after October 1940 changed its name to the Jewish Organization for Social Care (*Żydowskie Towarzystwo Opieki Społecznej* – in Yiddish it was known as *Aleynhilf*). Rachel Auerbach played an active role in its work. It was the only Jewish body whose activities covered the whole of the General-Government and until the entry of the United States into the war continued to receive funds from the Joint Distribution Committee. It attempted, above all, to use its resources to aid those sections of the population – refugees, starving children – who were neglected by the Social Welfare Department of the Judenrat, which, under German orders, was forced to favour 'active' and 'productive' sections of the population.

The Self-help Organization operated on two levels – legal and clandestine. Thus it used part of its funds to aid the underground and also held illegal classes and set up youth groups for children in the soup kitchens it organized. Similarly, through the Society for the Encouragement of Agriculture (Toporol), it sent Jewish youngsters, many of them youth movement activists, to do seasonal work on farms around Warsaw. Perhaps its most important activity was in the maintenance of soup kitchens, in which Rachel Auerbach was involved, although its ability to do this diminished as its funds dried up.

It also gave financial support to the underground archive, *Oyneg Shabes*. The creation of this archive was a characteristic feature of resistance in the ghetto. The Jews in Nazi-occupied Europe were determined to record all aspects of the tragic ordeal they were undergoing. According to Emanuel Ringelblum, the *spiritus movens* of the archive, 'Everyone wrote – journalists,

16 Henryka Lazowert was deported to Treblinka during the great deportation and perished there. For the full text of the poem see Yitzhak Zuckerman, M. Basuk (eds), *Sefer milkhamot hagetaot Beyn hahomot, hemakhanot, beya'arot* (Tel Aviv, 1947), 90.
17 Rachel Auerbach, *Behutsot Varshe 1939-1943* (Tel Aviv, 1954), II, 658.
18 Ringelblum, *Ksovim*, II, 232.

authors, teachers, social activists, young people, even children.'[19] They wrote for posterity. According to another of the members of the underground archive, Menahem Kon:

> I consider it a sacred duty for everyone, scholarly or not, to write down everything that he has seen or heard from those who witnessed the murderous actions committed by the barbarians in every Jewish settlement, so that, when the time comes – as it surely will – the world will read and learn what they have done. This will be the richest material for the lamenter who will write the elegy of our times; it will be the most potent inspiration for those who will avenge our sufferings.[20]

The last words recorded in the diary of Chaim Kaplan before he was deported to his death in Treblinka were, 'If I die – what will become of my diary?'[21]

Along with Ringelblum himself, the *Oyneg Shabes* group included many leading communal activists and writers, including Rachel Auerbach, Shmuel Winter, Eliyahu Gutkowski, Hirsch Wasser, Menahem Kon and Rabbi Shimon Huberband. Conscious of the momentous times in which they lived and of the deadly peril facing the Jews of Europe, they determined to chronicle all aspects of life in the ghetto to serve as a record for future generations. Its members were conscious of their terrible responsibility. Ringelblum described the organization as follows:

> The members of *Oyneg Shabes* have constituted and still constitute a homogeneous body, ruled by a single spirit and pervaded by a single idea. Oyneg Shabes is not an association of scholars who compete and strive against each other. It is a single entity, a brotherhood where all help each other and strive to achieve a common goal...
>
> Every member of *Oyneg Shabes* knows that his devoted labour and effort, the severe hardships he undergoes, the risks he takes 24 hours a day while engaged in the undercover work of carrying documents from place to place – all are undertaken for an exalted ideal and that in the days of freedom to come, society will know how to evaluate his contribution and will reward it with the highest honours available in liberated Europe. Oyneg Shabes is a fellowship, a fraternal order on

19 Ibid., 318.
20 Ringelblum Archive, part 1, no. 175, reprinted in J. Kermish (ed.), *To Live with Honor and Die with Honor: Selected Documents from the Warsaw Ghetto Underground Archives* (OS) (Oneg Shabbath) (Jerusalem, 1986), 24.
21 *The Warsaw Diary of Chaim A. Kaplan*, diary entry for 4 August 1942, 400.

> whose banner is inscribed its members' willingness to dedicate themselves completely to their cause and keep faith with each other in the service of the community.[22]

As its name implies (a reference to the Jewish custom of celebrating the end of the Sabbath) the *Oyneg Shabes* directorate met weekly on Saturday evening to exchange news and information. Its archives were buried in a number of milk churns and tin chests, some of which were found after the war, in September 1946 and December 1950, largely at the insistence of Rachel Auerbach. According to the diarist Abraham Lewin, who died in Treblinka but whose diary was found in the archive:

> In these tragic times, whenever several Jews gather together and each recounts just a part of what he has heard and seen, it becomes a mountain or a swollen sea of misfortune and Jewish blood. Jewish blood pure and simple. We gather every Sabbath, a group of activists in the Jewish community, to discuss our diaries and writings. We want our sufferings, these 'birth-pangs of the Messiah', to be impressed upon the memories of future generations and the memory of the whole world.[23]

What did they record? Lewin provides very characteristic examples of what is to be found in these diaries. He stressed the all-pervasive fear in which the inhabitants of the ghetto lived:

> An unremitting insecurity, a never-ending fear, is the most terrible aspect of all our tragic and bitter experiences. If we ever live to see the end of this cruel war and are able as free people and citizens to look back on the war years that we have lived through, then we will surely conclude that the most terrible and unholy, the most destructive aspect for our nervous system and our health was to live day and night in an atmosphere of unending fear and terror for our physical survival, in a continual wavering between life and death a state where every passing minute brought with it the danger that our hearts would literally burst with fear and dread. (16 May)[24]

22 Ringelblum, *Ksovim*, II, 102. An English version of Ringelblum's account of *Oyneg Shabes* can be found in Kermish, *To Live with Honor and Die with Honor,* 2, 21. It is dated correctly as late December, while the Warsaw published version in Yiddish is dated as late January.
23 Lewin, *A Cup of Tears*, diary entry for 6 June 1941, 120.
24 Ibid., 73.

As we know from Jürgen Becker's novel *Jacob the Liar* (English translation, New York 1975), the ghetto lived on hope. This is documented well by Lewin.

> One of the most remarkable incidental phenomena seen in the present war is the clinging to life, the almost complete cessation of suicides. People are dying in vast numbers of the typhus epidemic, are being tortured and murdered by the Germans in vast numbers, but people do not try to escape from life. In fact just the contrary: people are bound to life, body and soul and want to survive the war at any price. The tension of this epoch-making conflict is so great that everybody, young and old, great and small, wants to live to see the outcome of this giant struggle, and the new world order. Old men have only one wish: to live to see the end and to survive Hitler.
>
> I know an old Jew, grey with age, about 80 years old. He is an old man who was hit by a terrible misfortune last winter: he had an only son aged 52 who died of typhus. He had no other children. The son is dead. He hadn't remarried and had lived together with his son. A few days ago I visited the old man. As I was saying goodbye to him (he is still in complete command of his faculties) he burst into tears and said to me: 'I want to live to see the end of the war and then live for just another half hour longer.'
>
> We may well ask: what has such an old man to live for? But he does have something: he too wants to live 'for just half an hour' after the last shot is fired and this is the passionate desire of all Jews. (5 June)[25]

Lewin tried to distinguish between 'good' and 'bad' Germans, but increasingly cried out against the pervasive inhumanity. Not surprisingly, since he was a schoolteacher, it was the murder of children which above all aroused his wrath:

> There is no greater crime, no greater savagery than the murder of young and innocent children. The blood of our children will never be erased from the mark of Cain of the German people. Only now in these days have I come to appreciate and understand Bialik's song of anguish and rage: 'The Slaughter'. I must confess that, though I am one of Bialik's most fervent admirers, his 'In the Town of Murder' and 'The Slaughter', where there is such fiery talk of blood, murder and revenge, have never

25 Ibid., 119.

> been my favourites. I have always been drawn to his transcendent lyrics and his superb, brilliant epic poetry. But now I recall his cry from the heart: 'Accursed be he who cries out "Avenge this!" Vengeance for this, for the blood of a small child, the devil himself has not created'. Or 'If there is such a thing as justice, let it show itself now! But if only after my destruction, justice appears under the heavens, may its seat be destroyed for ever!' (25 May)[26]

But ultimately he rises above mere calls for revenge.

> Nowadays, death rules in all its majesty; while life hardly glows under a thick layer of ashes. Even this faint glow of life is feeble, miserable and weak, poor, devoid of any free breath, deprived of any spark of spiritual content. The very soul, both in the individual and in community, seems to have starved and perished, to have dulled and atrophied. There remains only the needs of the body; and it leads merely an organic-physiological existence...
>
> Yet, we wish to live on, to continue as free and creative men. This shall be our test. If, under the thick layer of ashes our life is not extinguished, this will prove the triumph of the human over the inhuman and that our will to live is mightier than the will to destruction; that we are capable of overcoming all evil forces which attempt to engulf us.[27]

From the beginning of the occupation the Nazis had attempted to terrorize the Jewish population. In November 1939, after a fracas in which a Jewish criminal killed a Polish policemen, they executed 53 men who lived in the building where the murder took place. In response to the actions of one Andrzej Kott, the son of Jewish converts who was active in Polish underground activity, the Gestapo arrested and then murdered over 200 Jews, mostly members of the intelligentsia in January 1940. Yet, in spite of the atmosphere of terror, soon around the Self-help Organization and the *Oyneg Shabes* group, political activity began to develop, partly under the stimulus of Emanuel Ringelblum. Ringelblum himself has described the informal discussions which developed:

> The war confronted the Jewish public circles with crucial questions. It was imperative to abandon the prewar political relationships and forge

26 Ibid., 96-7.
27 'Eulogy Read at a Commemorative Evening in Honour of Yitshak Meir Weissenberg, 13 September 1941', reproduced in Lewin, *A Cup of Tears*, 244.

> a united front from right to left: Hitler's campaign against the Jewish population bore the stamp of annihilation. It was directed against all strata and classes of Jewish society. For Hitlerism, there was no difference between a Zionist and a Bundist; both were hated to the same degree. It wanted to destroy them both. Thus it was necessary to define the course of struggle for the Jewish public...The institution of consultation by all the parties across the political spectrum was not defined by name, but it became a permanent body whose opinion was solicited by the Judenrat, the Self-help Organization, and more than once by the community as well.[28]

It did not prove an easy task to overcome the bitter divisions of pre-war years. In addition, disputes over whether the political objectives to be pursued should be relief, cultural development or political resistance soon surfaced and rapidly became more acute.

Yet, already at this time, an ominous change had come over German policy. The invasion of the Soviet Union in June 1941 was accompanied by the notorious *Kommissarbefehl*, empowering German commanders to shoot out of hand any Soviet commissar who fell into their hands, and by the creation of mobile killing squads (*Einsatzgruppen*). These followed the advancing German troops and were given the task of murdering Jews as well as communist officials. In the six months between June and December 1941, nearly a million Jews perished at the hands of these squads. It was at this time that the fateful decision was taken, in which Hitler was almost certainly personally involved, to 'solve' the Jewish problem by mass murder. The use of killing squads was abandoned, since the murder of women and children had affected troop morale and instead it was decided to use the technique of gassing, which had already been employed in the Nazi 'euthanasia' programme. Carbon monoxide was initially used, at first in the camp of Chełmno on the Ner and subsequently in the camp at Bełżec. By the spring of 1942, the technology of using an insecticide, Zyklon B, had developed and was employed in three additional camps, two created specifically for this purpose, Treblinka and Sobibor and one, Majdanek, where mass-murder was carried out but which was also used for holding Soviet prisoners-of-war and Polish prisoners. By the end of 1942, another political camp, that at Auschwitz in Silesia was also adapted for mass murder.

The blow was not long in falling on Warsaw. From early July rumours of impending deportation circulated widely in the ghetto. On 20 July, when arrangements for its implementation had already been completed the German

28 Ringelblum, *Ksovim*, II, 109.

authorities, in order to lull the population into a false sense of security, assured Czerniaków, head of the Judenrat, that these were entirely without foundation. The following day, many hostages, including *Judenrat* members or their wives, were seized and a number of individuals were shot. On 22 July at first light, Polish police, augmented by Ukrainian, Latvian and Lithuanian troops, sealed the exits from the ghetto. At ten o'clock, SS Major Herman Höfle appeared at the Judenrat. According to the diary of Czerniaków, who killed himself the following day:

> We were told that all the Jews, irrespective of sex and age, with certain exceptions, will be deported to the East. By 4 p.m. today a contingent of 6,000 people must be provided. And this (at a minimum) will be the daily quota... *Sturmbahnführer* Höfle [*Beauftragter* in charge of deportation] asked me to his office and informed me that for the time being my wife was free, but if the deportation were impeded in any way; she would be the first one to be shot as a hostage.[29]

For the next seven weeks, with a brief intermission between 28 August and 2 September, the Nazis deported daily between 2,000 and 10,000 people from the ghetto. They were first assembled at the Umschlagplatz, a square on the outskirts of the ghetto, and from there sent by train to Treblinka, where they were gassed with carbon monoxide from the exhausts of lorries. The deportation culminated in the comprehensive *Selektion* which lasted from 6 to 10 September, called the cauldron (Yiddish: *kesl*; Polish: *kocioł*) because it was carried out in so confined an area. During these days all Jews left in the ghetto were compelled to leave their homes and assemble in the streets adjacent to the Umschlagplatz. All those not part of the quota allocated to recognized workplaces were deported to Treblinka. The German plan was for 35,000 such slave labourers to remain in the ghetto. The final stages of this Selektion took place on the Day of Atonement, 21 September, when the Jewish policemen and their families were deported. The ghetto police was now reduced to 380 men. In all, according to German statistics, 235,741 people were deported to their deaths. (This is probably an underestimate.) In addition, more than 10,000 died or were shot in the violence accompanying the Aktion, another 12,000 were sent to labour camps and 8,000 sought refuge on the 'Aryan' side. As well as the slave labourers left in the ghetto, another 20,000-25,000 Jews remained there in hiding.

29 Czerniaków, Warsaw Diary, 385. On the great deportation, see Gutman, *The Jews of Warsaw*, pp. 197-233; S. Piotrowski, *Misja Odyla Globocnika* (Warsaw, 1949); Kermish, *To Live with Honor and Die with Honor*, pp. 691-716; Y. Arad, *Operation Reinhard* (Indianapolis, 1987).

Even at this stage, many of those deported thought they would be forced to undertake hard labour in the East and it was only gradually that those in the ghetto became aware of the true fate of the deportees. This issue can be clearly documented in Lewin's diary. Lewin sedulously noted all rumours which suggested that deportation might not mean death, among them many letters which were sent back to the ghetto. These letters were probably partly genuine messages from individuals who had escaped from trains to Treblinka, but feared to reveal this, partly the result of the conscious spreading of false rumours by the Germans and partly the creation of Poles who hoped in this way to persuade the inhabitants of the ghetto to send money and goods to dependents in the country, many of whom were probably no longer alive. Well informed as he was, Lewin soon became aware that there was no substance to the false hopes they aroused. On 6 August, he records that deportees were being sent to Treblinka which was 'the place of execution.' The following day he refers to 'the crematorium near Malkinia and Sokolow,' which was in all probability Treblinka, while on 9 August he observes grimly, 'It is clear that 99 per cent of those transported are being taken to their deaths.' He was soon, like all members of the *Oyneg Shabes* group, in possession of much more detail. On 11 August, he wrote:

> Smolar rang Sokołów. He was told that those that are deported, or if they are deported to Tr. are going to their 'death'. The news that K. brought. In Warsaw there is a Jew by the name of Slawa who has brought reports of Treblinka. Fifteen kilometres before the station at Treblinka the Germans take over the train. When people get out of the train they are beaten viciously. They are then driven into huge barracks. For five minutes heartrending screams are heard, then silence. The bodies that are taken out are swollen horribly. One person cannot get their arms round one of these bodies, so distended are they. Young men from among the prisoners are the gravediggers, the next day they too are killed. What horror![30]

Even more information was provided on 28 August by Dowid Nowodworski, a member of the leftwing Zionist youth movement *Hashomer Hatsair*, who managed to escape from the camp:

> Today we had a long talk with Dowid Nowodworski, who returned from Treblinka. He gave us the complete story of the sufferings that he endured from the first moment that he was seized to the escape from

30 Lewin, *A Cup of Tears*, 148-53.

Lodzia Hamersztajn and Ester Fiks ('Julcia') after the liberation. Both were couriers in the Jewish underground. Julcia's younger brother survived on the Aryan side of Warsaw

the death camp and up to his return to Warsaw. His words confirm once again and leave no room for doubt that all the deportees, both those who have been seized and those who reported voluntarily, are taken to be killed and that no one is saved. This is the naked truth, and how terrible, when we remember that in the last weeks at least 300,000 Jews have been exterminated, from Warsaw and other towns: Radom, Siedlce, and many, many others. From his words we put together a testimony of such stark anguish, so shattering, that it cannot be grasped and put into words. This is without doubt the greatest crime ever committed in the whole of history...

God! Are we really to be exterminated down to the very last of us? Now it is certain that all those deported from Warsaw have been killed.[31]

Thus, it became known from quite early on, at least among the politically active Jews in the ghetto that deportation meant death. Underground political activity, with the goal of undertaking armed resistance was discussed in the ghetto on 23 July, 1942, the day after the beginning of the great deportation by the representatives of the major political parties in the ghetto. On this occasion, when the implications of deportation were still unclear, the consensus was not to attempt armed resistance. Attitudes changed when more information became available and also as a result of the widespread shame felt at the failure to respond to the deportation in the summer of 1942 to the large majority of the ghetto's inhabitants. Two underground partisan organizations, the Jewish Combatant Organization and the Jewish Fighting Union were now formed, which are described in the essay on Rachel Auerbach.

When the Nazis attempted to begin deporting Jews on 18 January 1943, these organizations offered resistance. The Germans, astonished at the resistance they encountered, responded with a massive use of force. After several days, and the removal of about 6,500 people from the ghetto, they halted the deportation. They returned on 19 April, intending to destroy the ghetto entirely. In response, 650 inadequately-armed young men and women, 500 from the Jewish Fighting Organization and around 150 from the Jewish Military Union, began the first major action of Jewish resistance against the Nazis.

Their bravery, camaraderie, and the terrible price they paid, are described by Rachel Auerbach in the following pages published – for the first time – in English.

31 Ibid., 170.

The Jewish Revolt: Warsaw, 1943

RACHEL AUERBACH

I

Monday, April 19, 1943. Passover Eve, 5703.

German professors made note of these dates years before, so that every holiday could be wrecked, all Jewish festivals transformed into days of panic and pain.

But this time they inadvertently helped to deepen an ancient symbol and make Passover a memorial to Jewish liberation all over again.

Condemned to death, locked up in a walled-off ghetto, deprived of all their rights, isolated, debased, cut off from the world around them – in the face of certain annihilation, these Jews found the courage to launch an armed struggle against an enemy one hundred times stronger. The courage to embody the most urgent rights of the Jewish masses to human and national life, their belief in the future of their people, their faith in the coming victory of freedom and justice – at the moment of their own death.

Passover Eve, 1943 – the date of the third and final murder-assault on the Jews of Warsaw. Also, the date of the Jewish revolt – the Jewish rising.

The Passover sacrifice would be burned alive this time.

So let us once more tell the story of those great and frightful weeks from the beginning.

Let us list the facts, one after the other, recite them in brief like a chronicle of our hearts, like a *megillah*, a scroll to be read anew every year.

Let us go in sequence.

II

Hitler's war against the Jews was nearing its end.

Tens of thousands dead from hunger and epidemics lay in mass graves, millions in the vast burial ground that reached from one end of Poland to the other.

They were killed singly and in groups, ripped apart by dogs, beaten with clubs, tortured in camps of every type. Shot execution-style, the wounded buried along with the dead. Suffocated in gas vans, poisoned and asphyxiated in gas chambers, burned alive in enormous mass graves.

Millions....

The legacy of this robbery and murder had already been sorted and packed into thousands of freight cars bound for Germany.

Along with the hair cut from women's heads before their deaths and the teeth torn from the mouths of the dead.

The murderers were about to dig up the corpses and burn them.

Hitler's victories at the front had come to an end.

It was time to cover their tracks.

Himmler gave the order after Stalingrad: "Stop the mass murder!

"Transfer those Jews still living to camps and make use of their free labour for a while longer.

"And then exterminate them.

"Make the area *judenrein.*[1]

"Torch the ghettoes or rip down the buildings.

"Do not leave a trace.

"Not a trace."

III

The first assault on the Jews of Warsaw, the *Grossaktion* or Great Deportation of July 22 to September 13, 1942, was almost completely successful.

The enemy's proven tactics defeated all of Warsaw's preparations.

The Jewish political parties were now taking the first steps in coming together for the struggle.

Over 300,000 Warsaw Jews – among the bravest, most resolute, most vital people on earth – had been deported and killed with scarcely any attempt at collective resistance.

Only the commander of the Jewish militia was wounded. Only a couple of incidents of arson, a few acts of sabotage, took place.

Even though so much sorrow and pain, so much power, still lay coiled within the masses.

Even though a small faction acted entirely differently in far worse conditions only half a year later.

Even though...even though...

People started speaking openly about Treblinka[2] after the first deportation was over, once the heinous deception, the inner numbness, had worn off a little.

The genocide was four-fifths over by then.

The liquidation of the last seventy thousand-odd Jews still in the ghetto, legally or not, would be neither so easy nor so simple.

1 Jew-free.

2 Nazi death camp in south-east Poland where the Warsaw Jews were sent.

IV

The unification of the Jewish political factions that had been developing and taking shape before the catastrophe occurred virtually overnight. A couple of weeks after the first *Aktion*[3] in mid-October 1942. The Combat Organization was built by joining forces.

Though secret, the Combat Organization was the organized expression of the popular will, the nucleus of a comprehensive popular movement. Arming for self-defence – for insurrection – was now the essence of all activity in the ghetto.

The tragic shock of Treblinka unleashed a powerful energy in the ghetto. The agony balled up inside every Jew – their yearning for the dead, their terror at the murders, their hatred for the killers – found an outlet and a target. On the ruins of their lives, on the edge of destruction, this tiny remnant of a vast community underwent an extraordinary revolution and renewal.

Its dramatic conclusion was in keeping with the rich and stormy history of Jewish national and political life in Poland.

Stubborn and powerful as the Jewish fight against hunger and despair had been before the deportations, the fight against actual annihilation was no less stubborn and inexorable.

More dynamic, more elemental.

Jews no longer sat and waited to be taken off for "resettlement in the east." They stopped chasing desperately after the panacea of German stamps and documents, stopped jumping around like puppets on strings of German orders.

These Jews already knew the *truth*.

This mass fury found its earliest expression in a fever of work.

The ghetto that had been carved up – divided into separate zones with its hands and feet tied, subject every minute to a fresh attack – was transformed into a virtual fortress over the course of a couple of months: hundreds upon hundreds of *underground dwellings and hiding places for the Jewish population*, devised with Jewish ingenuity and organized by family or neighbourhood syndicates.

Water pipes and wells, sewage systems, electricity, ventilation, even radio sets in some places...All of them had medications, weeks' or months' worth of food, lighting and, above all, weapons...large sums of money, fortunes collected from the abandoned apartments.

3 Deportation.

A system of underground tunnels, corridors, outlets to the sewer system, to paths leading out of the ghetto to the Polish side.

Disguises...Stockpiles of disguises.

Above ground, the buildings were connected by holes in the walls, passageways in the attics.

There were snipers' nests in some of the houses, observation posts, little factories for hand grenades and other explosives. These were the Combat Organization bases. There were also private initiatives for arming the bunkers. Solid citizens were buying pistols and dreaming of higher calibre guns. Most bunkers had a regular watch and an elected commander. An established disciplinary routine. Observation posts would be set up during the revolt, regular tours of duty established. Private, "wild" defence operations were under the Combat Organization's influence.

All the necessary materials had to be smuggled into the ghetto. The smuggling happening now was even braver and more ingenious than it had been in the past.

Out went fabrics and clothing, machine parts, anything of value in daily Polish life. In came nothing but what could be used for defence: revolvers and grenades, ammunition and machine pistols. Dynamite and potash mixtures, gasoline and nitroglycerine...Jews hid money in glucose and vitamin capsules, in flour and kasha, in sugar and beans, in bottles of carrot juice and the bottles of Molotov cocktails.[4]

Jewish weapons, Jewish defence.

A source of strength:

The camaraderie of the Jewish parties. The sincere, if temporary, renunciation of animosity. Intramural harmony and national unity.

A source of courage and pathos, the secret and basis of their communal power.

V

The Jewish Combat Organization had already made its debut – armed resistance during the four-day deportation *Aktion* in January. The first few dozen Germans killed and wounded in the ghetto. The Organization's significance for people in the ghetto continued to grow.

The entire membership had already been mobilized and was quartered in collective apartments. Divided into squadrons according to party. The block units were multi-party, under a shared commander. The administration, in

4 Molotov cocktail was the name given to the liquid inside the homemade explosive bottles. The term appears to have originated in the partisan movement.

which all parties were represented, was in the Central Ghetto.[5]

There were virtually no members of the military in the Organization. Will and spirit were what mattered. They learned the rest with great zeal: use of weapons, adaptation to conditions of struggle in the ghetto. The fine art of mastering fear...

An operation to cleanse the ghetto of traitors and enemy agents. Acts of sabotage against the German firms. Expropriations for the sake of armaments.

Other Jews contributed generously to help the "Party",[6] which was the terror of all the informers and collaborators, the pride and joy of all the other Jews.

The Organization watched over the ghetto. It was always prepared.

The Germans knew what was going on in the ghetto but were not able to take control of the situation by conventional means.

The gendarmes on the watch were bribed. The police units show their cowardice during the January *Aktion*. They could no longer rely on their terrorized Jewish collaborators. They wanted to empty the nest of insubordination "amicably", without suffering any casualties of their own. They tried using hypocritical mildness to lure the Jews to the labour camps of Poniatówa and Trawniki.[7]

But the Jews paid no more attention to German promises. They followed the guidelines issued by the Organization. They stayed where they were and kept building their fortress.

"Indescribable chaos reigned in the ghetto," as one German general wrote about this time. "There were Jewish bunkers and ammunition factories even in the German military factories."

O, it wasn't the chaos that he thought it was. A highly developed, cleverly organized operation.

The Germans had nothing with which to manufacture any illusions. And the Jews had nothing left with which to illude themselves.

The Germans were preparing a new *Aktion*.

The Jews were preparing for battle.

5 Following the first deportation *Aktion*, the ghetto was sequestered and divided into several separate work- and living-areas for the Jews working for German firms. The Central Ghetto was located in the quadrilateral between Gęsia, Franciskańska, Smocza, Stawki, and Bonifraterska Streets where, in addition to the remaining *Judenrat* institutions and certain German firms, the dwellings of Jews taken to work on the Polish side were also located.

6 The popular name for the Combat Organization and the underground movement in general among both Jews and Poles.

7 These labour camps were located in the Lublin area.

VI

The resistance movement in the occupied eastern territories increased in the wake of Stalingrad. The terror had intensified and so had the resistance.

The struggle of the other occupied peoples had plenty of room to breathe. The White Russian, Ukrainian, and Polish partisan and underground armies were able to prepare for their final act when conditions were right and the front had drawn near.

The Jewish organization had to enter the fray *now*, with its last and its best. With almost no chance of success.

If it didn't, it wouldn't live to join the struggle.

Young people took the yoke of national action, of national policy, upon themselves. The youngest among them were the first to be ready to act.

And some young Jews came back from the Polish side and from the forests to fight and die in the ghetto.

Cut off from any back-up, utterly isolated, the underground Jewish army – the weakest, militarily, of them all – had to be the very first to engage in urban warfare.

Others were able to learn from its courage and example, its experiences and innovations.[8] Condemned from its very founding to physical defeat, it was supposed to win the highest moral victory.

"We have to fight now. We are ready to die for the dignity of our people and mankind..."

This was their programme, as formulated in an official document, an appeal to officials of the Polish government-in-exile.[9]

"Let us die with honour," was the final motto on the call to arms posted in the ghetto on the last night.

The night before Passover, the night before the revolt.

VII

Sunday, April 18, 1943

Military units deployed in Warsaw.

One detachment SS *Panzergrenadiers* – 400 men, 6 officers

8 During the general uprising, the Polish fighters in the old city used the sewers for military movements. The apartment houses were organized into interlinked complexes. These methods and others were first tried out in the ghetto. There was a Jewish detachment fighting in the old city.

9 The Polish government-in-exile was in London. The appeal was for help in procuring arms. The Combat Organization's chief negotiator was Mordechai Tenenbaum (Tamaroff), later commander of the Bialystok Ghetto uprising.

One reserve detachment of SS cavalry – 450 men, 10 officers
One detachment police – 126 men, 6 officers
One detachment *Sonderdiens*[10] – 48 men, 2 officers
Ukrainian auxiliaries – 151 men
Security police – 55 men
Polish police – 471 men plus officers
Units and equipment allocated by the *Wehrmacht*:
Four cannons with crews
One flamethrower
One detachment of pioneers – 16 men, 2 officers
One detachment of medics with ambulance
One eight-wheeled French armoured car with crew.
Two German tanks – armoured infantry vehicles with crews
Later additions:
Polish firefighters – 166 men with equipment
One artillery battery with crew.
Special sapper-combat engineer divisions to plant mines and carry out explosions

The strength of the other detachments would be increased.

In short:

An army. Soldiers, officers, n.c.o.'s, fully trained and fully equipped, an army standing ready to storm the ghetto fortress.

Its commander, an eminent man in his field, was also in Warsaw – Jürgen Stroop, *Brigadeführer* and *Generalmajor* of Police, picked for the job by Himmler himself.

11 a.m:

A conference of SS and police leaders from the Warsaw district.

A staff meeting to discuss details in advance of an offensive.

News from the Polish side reached the ghetto that evening.

The alarm spread across the ghetto and shop [German factory] zones.

It grew stronger.

The Combat Organization held a staff meeting, too, with representatives of all its groups. Final orders were issued.

The whole ghetto was on its feet.

The night before Passover.

Our mothers and grandmothers used to be up late that night – there was bedding still to be changed, scrubbing and koshering to be done. Our fathers went around with feather dusters and candles, whisking little slices of bread

10 Special services, i.e. auxiliary police.

together in wooden spoons to fulfil the commandment to get rid of all leaven.

The ghetto was up.

Families carried packs, moved into bunkers. Men were wandering the courtyards despondently. The windows were blacked out, but life, severely wounded, buzzed on in buildings and cellars. People whispered.

Midnight:

The Combat Organization emerges from underground.

The curfew is no longer in force. With guns in their hands, clad in German uniforms and helmets, a couple of patrols set out into the ghetto.

They stride through the streets, banging at gates like soldiers. The gates open fearfully; the soldiers are recognized with a stab of pain followed by enthusiasm. "Oh, they're Jews, our boys. Oh, fighters!"

A chapter of Polish and of Warsaw history is spreading through the streets and courtyards of the ghetto, a chapter of Jewish history.

O, Jewish Insurrection!

They waken, they warn. They call for revolt. The manifesto of the uprising already hangs on the walls of the ghetto.[11]

The last call to the last struggle ends with the motto:

"Fight, die, for the honour of our people."

2 a.m.

The ghetto is besieged. For the third and last time. Besieged.

The walls are a kilometre long and three metres high. Every twenty-five metres, a gendarme or "blue" policeman, armed with rifles.

The circle was now closed.

A few minutes after two, the Combat Organization's groups assume their positions.

At four German infantry and motorized detachments started to enter through the outer gates, followed by trucks, supplies, ambulances. Small groups went as far as no-man's land, the uninhabited area between the ghetto and the shop zones, where they began to form into units.

They had been ordered to maintain silence. Their engines hummed at half-throttle.

Their precautions are vain; the ghetto isn't sleeping. The ghetto is listening to the steps of those who creep around the walls like thieves, like bandits.

Like bands of marauders bent on plunder.

Killing like beasts of prey, unsheathing their nails.

11 *Insurekcja* and *manifest* – terms from the first Polish uprising in 1794, led by Tadeusz Kósciuszko.

The gate to the Central Ghetto at Gęsia and Zamenhof Streets.

They start marching in.

VIII

There was a small space just left of the gate, in front of the *Judenrat* building at Zamenhof 19.

The troops split into two columns. One went straight up Zamenhof, while the other went right, along the wall that divided the even numbers on Gęsia from the odd. Each was welcomed a few minutes later.

At the intersection of Mila and Nalewki, from every corner where Mila and Zamenhof meet.

There were two groups of masked fighters hiding in the buildings at 29, 31 and 33 Nalewki. They let the enemy draw near, then suddenly opened fire from every aperture, hurling grenades and Molotov cocktails.

The enemy troops flung themselves to the ground. Half of them stood up, the dead or wounded were left lying. The survivors returned fire, showering the three buildings with a hail of machine gun bullets.

The fire fight went on for two hours. Then – the Germans retreated.

The first battle, the first Jewish victory.

The Germans returned two hours later. They put up a barricade at the intersection of Nalewki and Franciskańska and set fire to the three buildings. Jews set fire to a *Werterfassung*[12] storeroom on the ground floor. A Molotov cocktail left the barricade in flames. The fight went on. The Jews held their position for six full hours, retreating only in the face of the flames, without a single casualty.

The second German column at Zamenhof and Mila suffered an even worse defeat. Concentric Jewish fire from all four sides at once, from every attic and upper floor...The Germans didn't always manage to shoot back. The Jews saw their enemies lying in pools of blood. They saw a German whose uniform had caught fire from a Molotov cocktail.

The rest scattered into the business entrances and courtyard gates of nearby buildings, afraid to stick their heads out.

8 a.m.

General Stroop appears in the square by the *Judenrat* and assumes command.

12 *Werterfassung* referred to disposing of the property of the murdered or deported Jews for the benefit of the Germans.

SS Brigadefuehrer and Majorgeneral of Police Jürgen Stroop

It doesn't have much effect.

First, he sends a *Panzer* detachment for the insurrectionist nest at Zamenhof and Mila, a heavy armoured vehicle followed by two lighter tankettes.

And behold! Boys who until today had had nothing to do with heavy weapons, most of whom were using arms for the very first time, were not fazed at all. They had enough *sang froid* to let the tank draw close enough for their Molotov cocktails to reach it. Their aim was true; the armoured car caught fire. Explosions, dead and burned Germans. The enemy scarcely managed to withdraw with its other two armoured cars, which were still behind them; the soldiers who had been hiding in the doorways were hiding between them.

They ran away.

The new second-hand clothing business in Warsaw, the war haberdasheries of Nalewki and Świętojerska, the war industry of ghetto Jewish home-workers, had proven itself good for something. It had just passed the quality test.

One after the other, the dead and wounded Germans were being carried off from the intersection of Gęsia and Nalewki.

The only first aid station was overwhelmed. Alarms went out for ambulances, which were blaring their way through the streets.

Great as the catastrophe was for the Germans, the shame was even greater. They would try to convince their superiors and the Polish population that the shooting came from Polish bandits who were hiding in the ghetto, from German deserters who had joined up with them. Anything but the Jews...

Who were having their moment, enjoying the delights of victory for a brief forever...

Two hours later, Stroop decided to try again. He sent out another detachment, with orders to force their way through. But this time, too – an armed ambush from the attic of Zamenhof 29. As long as the enemy proceeded directly and in the open, the road that the Jewish boys were guarding would never be free.

Whether it suited him or not, the German general had to abandon his charge for the time being.

"The ghetto could not be taken in a frontal attack," a foreign commentator wrote afterwards. The Germans had to fall back on their technical superiority, on heavy weapons.

There was already an airplane circling the ghetto to observe and specify precise locations. Anti-aircraft guns were set up in the area outside the ghetto and started firing on the houses from which the Jews had been shooting.

There was nothing else for it. The five groups that had been fighting there, each representing a different party, started to retreat.

The Jews' "successful defence", as German military communications put it, "was not to be doubted." The "escape manoeuvres" across the attics to "previously prepared new bases" were accomplished without losses. The Jews lost a grand total of one fighter in the battle at Mila and Zamenhof.

The fighting on Muranowska Square also continued until noon. Here, too, there was likely a disabled tank, dead and wounded Germans. Here, too, the revolt remained uncrushed that day. Here, too, Stroop had to leave the follow-up for the morrow.

5:30 p.m.

More "unexpectedly strong resistance", this time on Franciskańska Street.

Echoes of the battle sounded anew across the whole of the city, across the Polish streets. People who had paid no attention to explosions or the rat-tat-tat of machine guns that morning now learned the truth. There were Jews hiding in their midst.

A hammer blow to the heart. Pain, mortal fear, rapture:

It's happening!

A great number of Jews was captured that day. Some were killed, some sent to camps. "Operations were broken off on account of gathering darkness."

So reads the first German report from the ghetto front. "Reinforced the guard around the walls outside the ghetto.

Seders were still held in the ghetto that Monday night, the first night of the uprising.

Deep in the bunkers, in desolate apartments where you took cover until there was a lull in the shooting, Jews sat down one last time at tables that had been set.

They recited the *Hagaddah.*[13]

And Pharaoh's evil deeds in Egypt blended with those of the wicked Hitler.

Moshe ben Eliezer,[14] Rabbi Joshua, Rabbi Elazar ben Azariah, and Rabbi Akiva...

Like the sages of Bnei Brak, the Jews of Warsaw recalled the miracles of the Exodus from Egypt that night and spoke of rebellion, praising what the young fighters of Mila and Zamenhof, Nalewki and Smocza, had done.

The evil one had to be destroyed like Pharaoh and his hosts.

Their longing for redemption was beyond imagination.

The same old tune, the same old words.

They knew that it was their destiny to die on the threshold of deliverance.

And they sang and they cried.

Old and young were united in imagination with their ancestors' fight for freedom. Some in the struggle for Jewish liberation and a land of their own, others with the liberation of all humanity.

There was a rabbi living at the time on Kurza (formerly Kupiecka, later Meiselsa) Street.

On the street of the Warsaw rabbi and friend of the Polish uprising of 1863, there now lived a different scholar with the same name: Meisels.

And he sent a message of love to the fighters.

Heartfelt blessings and bundles of matzoh.

One after the other, as if they were the students of Rabbi Akiva,[15] the fighters started to be mourned the next day. From the second day of Passover until Shavuos, those who sacrificed their young lives every day were commemorated

13 Jewish text that sets out the order of the Passover Seder.

14 The author seems to be quoting from memory here. According to the *Hagaddah*, the rabbis gathered that night in Bnei Brak were: Eliezer, Joshua, Elazar ben Azariah, Akiva, and Tarfon (trans.).

15 According to the Talmud (Yevomos 62b), 24,000 students of Rabbi Akiva died between Passover and Shavuos [Pentecost] because of their failure to treat one another with respect.

Smoking out the jews and bandits

with a mournful tune.

Oy, "It is sweet and beautiful to die for your people."

And the trams kept running that first day, across Bonifraterska to Żoliborz, along the ghetto wall. In houses and attics facing the ghetto, bold people looked inside. They said that they saw flags.

Blue and white, white and red, waving side by side.

A call to arms to the Jews, a battlefield greeting to the Poles.

True or not, it's a beautiful story.

A legend was starting to take shape in the mouths of the common people, a popular legend about the revolt of the Jews.

IX

The "shops"[16] come into the foreground during the next two days of the uprising. Only small groups had been deployed to the Central Ghetto, a few hundred Germans, who searched very carefully in burned out, demolished

16 German factories in the ghetto which employed Jews as workers.

Guarding Jews forced out of underground bunkers

buildings. They uncovered a few bunkers, dragged a few dozen Jews out here and there.

Before proceeding to complete annihilation, Stroop wanted to be rid of all kinds of "ordnance factories" that were getting in the way of the job he had to do, asking him to put out fires, to save their storerooms and machines from bullets and flames.

Stroop's order was, "Everything out – now!"

The German factory owners would have liked to obey. They had still not given up the attempt to turn the ghetto fires to their advantage. They tried to persuade the Jews that the *Aktion* was only meant to "cleanse" the Central Ghetto, that their blocks had been surrounded to keep "them" out.

The "bandits and criminals," the Jews of the Combat Organization.

But there was no need at all to let any "bandits" in from elsewhere. They were here, too, in every shop. They didn't even want to wait until it was time for them to defend themselves. Until such time as someone were to come for them, they were the attackers.

In the factories of Többens, both the Schultzes, Röhrich, Hallman, and Schilling; on Leszno, Nowolipie, Smocza and Nowolipke – everywhere. They stood ready from the night of the 19th, lurking, waiting for the signal, for their hour.

April 20th was the Führer's birthday. In dress uniforms, freshly shaved, buttons polished, the soldiers were marching into the ghetto to kill and torture Jews. The roll call that morning was festive.

They were afraid to set foot in the ghetto, but they were still on the other side of the wall, feeling safe.

At the intersection of Leszno and Żelazna, the columns split off to the right.

And our boys surprised the enemy a second time.

Grenades, bombs, Molotov cocktails were flung onto the troops from the attics and upper storeys of Leszno 36, 74 and 76, just as they were the day before.

Dead and wounded, covered in flames from the bottles that hit their helmets.

They had been seen in the same condition yesterday on Zamenhof St. On fire and running, jumping, waving their hands above their heads like lunatics.

"The Molotov cocktail is really something" thought the Jewish boys, who had probably never killed a chicken or anything else in their lives. They were thirsting for vengeance...

Well-timed bottles from the windows of Smocza 8 and 10 stopped a tank. It never made it to the battlefield.

On one of the following days, a two-kilogram bomb will be tossed into an armoured car full of troops in this area.

And once again, the joy of the fighters, boys and girls alike, will be great, almost childlike.

The pain and regrets of the group in that block.

They had, with considerable difficulty, laid two mines, one underneath the "command post" at Żelazna 103, the other under the pavement in front of Nowolipie 67, one of their bases, but they did not go off.

A fire fight broke out. The Germans and their Ukrainian auxiliaries were shooting, there were dead and wounded on both sides, but they were unable to cut the area off completely. Stroop left the "cleansing" for later. Here, too, the Jews were victorious, if only for a little while.

The battle at Świętojerska and Walowa started on Tuesday afternoon...

The brush-making shop, the last refuge for some of the social and political activists, a mental and physical reservoir for the combat movement.

Some of the different parties' best fighting groups were clustered here. They, too, had been standing ready since the first night. The enemy kept a more energetic watch on this area than on others. The facades of the buildings were lit up with reflectors at night, while the front windows were

Women and children are marched to the Umschlagplatz for deportation

under constant fire.

Talks about going to the labour camps came to nothing.

"The Jews are absolutely not inclined to leave the place" noted the German in his report. Between 2 and 3 p.m., he ordered the use of force.

A column of troops was approaching the gate of the building at the corner of Walowa and Franciskańska that led to the brush shop. The German watchman was unable to get it open. A mighty blast startled the whole area. The neighbouring houses were shaking. The ground opened up under the feet of the German soldiers in the centre of the column.

A mine had long been waiting and it did not disappoint.

There was an observation post on one of the floors of the building at Walowa 2, and it was here that the electric switch for the mine was kept. The boys were thus able to observe its effects. Bodies flying in the air; disembodied limbs; dead, dazed, and wounded, the Germans lay on the ground. A pitiful remnant was just able to stand up and limp back to where they came from with their heads hung low.

Look your fill at this sight, young fighters! Quicken your hearts for as long as you are able.

The alarm reached Stroop, who demanded that his soldiers carry their orders out to the letter. (How good it was for the Jews to be able to see their foes and fight them at close quarters).

Full of fear and caution, one by one, the soldiers spread themselves along the wall on Walowa and Świętojerska, hunched over, heads bowed, automatics in their hands.

A hail of bullets, grenades, Molotov cocktails. An army veteran takes aim and fires a rifle from an upper storey.

And just as yesterday in the Central Ghetto, a great number of fallen and wounded attackers, only a few casualties for the defence. Meanwhile, the Germans were not getting through...

Fewer than half the soldiers who had entered the block were left. Once again, they retreated.

Time was passing, evening was drawing nigh. Suddenly, the sound of a cannon splits the air. It's the 100 mm howitzer. Just as yesterday, Stroop is forced to fall back on heavy weapons. Three smaller cannons were also shooting at the shop zone. A machine gun was set up at the intersection of Nowiniarska and Franciskańska. Surrounded on all sides. Once the artillery had prepared the ground, a fresh assault was mounted from two sides at once.

A sizable group of stormtroopers broke through from Franciskańska Street and penetrated the buildings.

Once again the Jewish boys and girls were not fazed, not by the cannons,

Stroop demanded that his soldiers carry their orders out to the letter

not by the combat. They fought like soldiers...like soldiers. They didn't give in, though victim after victim was falling.

The struggle played out on stairs, in attics, by chimneys. Defenders were falling left and right. They had orders not to let themselves be caught between the two columns and they carried this order out. The Germans were driven from the attics.

A grotesque surprise on the street in front of the buildings: German politicians.

The German factory boss with SS officers. They have come to offer the Jews a "truce" so that they could clear away their dead and wounded and once again try to convince the Jews to be transported to Poniatówa.

They were wasting their time. The Jews didn't believe them and had no further desire to talk to Germans. They didn't stop shooting for a minute – from every building, every window, every floor. Men were shooting – and so were the women. The Germans were just noticing this for the very first time. They were stunned.

No, these Jews were not about to lay their miserable arms down voluntarily.

Early the next day, Stroop called in a special detachment of sappers and pioneers. There was no choice: the warehouses could not be saved.

They brought the necessary tools, dragged cans of gasoline. They carried out their orders like professionals, blowing up and burning down.

The block started burning on three sides at once.

The first big fire in the ghetto.

Hell was breaking loose.

...Scores of people driven from their hiding places, fleeing the flames at the last minute. People who knew neither how to save themselves nor which death to choose. Whole families leaping from upper floors. Escape attempts mingled with suicides...

The picture is clear.

Melted asphalt, even the glass blown from the windows by explosions: everything made of wood was burning, everything made of stone or iron was glowing with heat. No air to breathe, the heat itself could kill from a distance. Blackened bodies. A stench of burning flesh drifting with the wind.

The picture is complete. Soon the whole ghetto will look like this.

The combat unit in the brush shop had no intention of being burned alive. They tried to sneak out of their area that evening.

The groups come together, daring, bold, and well-organized. They break through the flames of the burning buildings, the ring of the siege.

An hour later they're occupying a new base of operations on Franciskańska St.

They left behind them a place of fire and terrifying disaster. The last of their nearest and dearest. Before them lay a landscape of fresh trials, of horror and pain.

They were determined to do what they had to until the end.

X

The first days of the fighting – days of Jewish victory in everything but name.

"The first week of the uprising bears the clear character of a military operation," wrote someone in a Polish report.

In nests concealed in upper storeys, window-niches, garrets, and fortified balconies...

Jews sat shooting.

Aspects of a city under attack.

At first the defender is more secure than the attacker.

The attacker has to show himself in the open, often without any cover. His tanks are being blown up or set afire. The defender also tends to know the terrain better.

It was the same in the ghetto. The only thing out of the ordinary was that our fighters – young, inexperienced, with no real military training – were able to make full use of both their defensive advantages. They attacked from above and defended their positions for as long as possible. They held every point until the last minute and almost always managed to retreat on time, with negligible losses, on paths that only they, the neighbourhood children, knew so well.

Up to now, everything was "natural".

Then there came the moment when everything gets difficult – different than it is with others.

It got to the point where others capitulate.

Not the Jews.

Unparalleled as the Jews' situation was, their bearing now was no less so.

Resistance, active and passive, until the end and even – beyond.

After the losses of men and equipment in the first two or three days, the Germans all but gave up on direct attacks on fortified positions.

Cannons, airplanes, heavy weapons, dynamite...

The enemy brought all of its technical advantages into play and enlisted the help of the elements: fire and water. It poisoned the air in the sewers.

Which Jew first came up with the idea of hiding in the sewers?...

And the days of fire and heavy weapons began.

The Germans no longer strode through the ghetto in massed ranks that were easy targets for Jewish attacks, but in smaller *Durchkämmungs Stosstruppen* that were here today, there tomorrow, and on some days, everywhere at once. Sometimes very early, sometimes not until 9, 10, or even 11 o'clock...so that the Jews would think that the *Aktion* had already ended, or at least been interrupted.

They spread false news, made use of elaborate contrivances, to keep the Jews in turmoil.

They combed the ghetto with an iron comb.

In order to drag out people who had squeezed into the ground, buried

Jews are led away from the burning ghetto by SS guards

themselves alive.

From time to time, a major assault on a given area. "A deployment of the main forces."

They distinguish themselves with what Stroop praises as "joy in deployment."

Joy...O, God...

Cannons, surveillance and bombs from the air. A raid on the sewers – gas and dynamite from below. The main weapon, though, was simple and old-fashioned, the least expensive and most effective: fire.

This great weapon combines with smaller and smaller ones: listening devices, tracking dogs.

The Jews can't get near any artillery emplacements. They have nothing with which to fight fires, let alone drive off airplanes.

The Golem of Technology is fighting for the Germans.

German soldiers will only approach a building that is burning or blown apart.

The Jews have to change their tactics. At times, it is utterly impossible for them to fight. They are also starting to run low on ammunition.

Nonetheless, the fight goes on. The revolt has not been crushed.

The ghetto is veiled in clouds of smoke and fire.

Grey, black, yellow, rust.

They hide the horizon for days, they hide our fighters.

And dazzle the wide-open, bulging eye.

Is someone still screaming through the roar? The firestorm buzzes on. Is someone still alive out there? Can someone there still fight?

There is a pole sticking out of the seething flames, redder and taller than the rest.

A new pillar of fire from a newly ignited house.

A pillar of fire...

It's them.

Louder than the other explosions.

Bloody, burning bits of news.

Straight from the most frightful of all battlefields.

They reach us weeks and months, sometimes years later.

We must collect them all, all the details.

Lest a single one be lost to our people's memory.

As Rome and Jerusalem burned, so did the ghetto, hemmed in on all sides by a wall and a threefold ring of enemies...

As powerful as Titus, as fabulous as Nero, they *had* to come out on top, these lords of so much disaster and destruction.

The directors and cast of the spectacle: General Stroop and his adjutants, who were tasteful enough to marvel at these events, to describe and photograph them.

There was no Flavius Josephus in the enemy camp, no one to undertake a day-by-day description of the Jewish war.

The enemy himself became the chronicler – Stroop, in his accounts and reports.[17]

There are deeds for which there are no longer any Jewish witnesses, facts that no Jew can any longer relate. They have been killed. Stroop is their reporter and photographer.

Where Jews no longer know what to say about the fight, the executioner takes the floor and delivers a testament to Jewish valour.

As the American prosecutor in Nuremberg said of Stroop's report, "The German general has created an unintentional epic of Jewish valour."

He was right.

It is also a document of Jewish suffering and death, a document of the unimaginable degeneracy and cruelty of the Germans.

It is an unwritten law of crime that tracks are going to be left. And it is the unwritten right of history to grab its tools wherever it can.

A calendar of the uprising can be assembled from contemporary and later reports, Jewish, Polish, and German.

Here is a dateline, with episodes.

Every date – the date of a mass drama. Every day, a year; every night, an apocalypse of red fire in the sky.

On one date, so many bunkers were uncovered; on another, so many more.

Every bunker had its story, human and tragic.

Every family, every person, a separate tragedy, self-contained, unlike any other. Who will write them down or read them through, these histories, these tragedies, these dramas?

Every chapter, every act – so similar and so different.

17 During the liquidation *Aktion*, General Stroop sent one or two teletypes a day to Senior SS and Police Commander Krüger in Cracow. Aside from that, he gave a general report to the Congress of SS and police leaders in occupied Poland on May 18. Both reports, as well as a 'photo report', came to light during his trial in Nuremberg. See the Stroop Report.

They combed the ghetto with an iron comb...to drag out people who had squeezed into the ground, buried themselves alive

April 22, Stroop:
"From so-called 'cleared' buildings...shooting at us all night...fifteen bunkers blown up...Jews scattered under the ruins...smoked out...houses set on fire (Świętojerska, Franciskańska, Muranów). Engulfed by flames, masses of Jews, entire families, leapt out the windows, tried to lower themselves with sheets that they had knotted together, to escape the fire. The Jews were worried that they and other Jews were going to be liquidated ... Another report of Jews living underneath the ghetto in the sewer pipes. This, alas, cannot be helped. Blocking the sewers off did not work. Unfortunately, the city management has no idea what to do about it. Meanwhile, pouring creosote into the water, putting *Nebelkerze*[18] in the sewers, is unfortunately even less effective.

"It must also be reported that we were fired upon from the Aryan side. We captured and liquidated thirty-five Poles. The Poles shouted slogans before their deaths.

"Captured, transported, shot – so-and-so many Jews.

"Plunder was seized.

18 Smoke grenades (trans.).

Every doorway is a fortress: a German artillery aims at a position held by Jewish fighters

Contacts with the *Wehrmacht* – perfect."

April 23, Stroop:
"3500 Jews captured, 200 shot, 48 bunkers blown up. Shooting from the guard at the wall. Houses were set afire – Jews were shooting from inside the buildings and from their balconies until the end. Guns...well-appointed bunkers...weapons and ammunition...gas masks, in one instance."
Polish-Jewish sources:
On the 23rd, a call to the Polish population:

"Poles, citizens, soldiers of freedom...There is a struggle taking place... Every doorway is a fortress...We might die...We will never surrender... Vengeance – for Auschwitz and Treblinka; Bełżec and Majdanek."[19]

On the 23rd, a letter from the commander in the ghetto. He was writing to his deputies.[20]

"No words can express what we have lived through...The dream has come true...Self-defence...Life in the ghetto now beggars description...Only individuals will survive...Farewell...We will meet again...Perhaps..."

19 Belzec and Majdanek were death camps.
20 The commander was Mordechai Anielewicz. His deputy, Yitzhok Zuckerman (Antek), was the Combat Organization's representative on the Polish side.

He gives notice of a shift to partisan tactics. The change is made. That night – regrouping...The activists are concentrated in several bunkers on Mila and Franciskańska. Fighting groups are assigned to other bunkers. To keep order, prevent panic, and protect. They will appear as soon as the Germans make their way to the houses.

Reconnaissance groups in the nights. Liaisons from group to group. Guard posts lurking in the ruins and watching from above, giving warning, signalling when to attack.

Panicked masses fleeing the Germans, fleeing the flames. And in the midst of this terror and calamity, they, the fighters, have the strength and courage to carry out operations, follow orders, execute plans...

April 24:
A group of Jewish fighters uncovered on Praga St. They defended themselves with Molotov cocktails and grenades, set fire to a German armoured car, wounded Germans, and – fell...Stubborn resistance today in the residential blocks of the ghetto. Fires. 274 Jews shot in combat.

April 25:
An order to evacuate the Jews from the Többens block on Leszno by noon. An ultimatum. Extended to 6 p.m. A few people report, the rest hide in bunkers. The local fighters toss grenades. Stroop writes: "Armed resistance." He writes: "If the sky over the ghetto was covered last night in a fiery gleam, today it is a giant sea of flames."

April 26:
"Thirty bunkers blown up. 362 rebel casualties. Resistance at every step... A house that was being burned down – a clandestine ammunition factory – flew up into the air..."

April 27:
Niska St. set on fire. Stroop writes: "They shot until the last second, then jumped from the upper storeys after throwing down cushions and mattresses, but only once the fire left them with no way out...115 Jews killed in combat."

A battle that day on "Aryan" Muranowska St, at number 2. 120 well-armed men who got there via a tunnel from Muranowska 5...Stroop writes: "SS uniforms, German helmets, even a machine gun. Set fire to the house, took care of twenty-four Jews in battle. They leapt from the burning windows and balconies, calling curses down on Germany and reviling the

Führer." Seventeen Poles were also killed for harbouring Jews and two Polish policemen for not informing on them...The conclusion of the battle had to be put off to the next day.

April 29:

An *Aktion* on Nowolipie and Nowolipki Streets in the Schilling, Hallman, and Schultz blocks...Deep bunkers, well-fortified and well-guarded. Got to one only after the house was demolished. "Stiff resistance. Countless Jews killed in the explosion. An ammunition storeroom flew into the air. Many guns and ammunition found in the bunkers, an even greater number of German uniforms and helmets."

On the same day a group of fighters left the Többens block via the sewer on Ogrodowa St., but only some escaped. Some even remained on Leszno. The Jews' use of the sewers was driving Stroop to distraction. He ordered a number of sewer outlets on the Polish side to be blown up or bricked over.

April 30:

The battle of Nowolipie-Nowolipki goes on. Stroop writes: "Had to use a cannon against one of the blocks." He becomes aware of the fact – which he finds interesting – that armed Jews were protecting the people from exposure, making sure that they didn't leave their bunkers even at night, lest they leave tracks. They concealed the exits from outside, enforced discipline with the barrel of a gun.

May 1:

A boundary marker, a pillar of fire in the history of the uprising. The inferno in the ghetto was reaching its peak. The Polish underground radio station, *Swit,*[21] reminded the fighting groups of the holiday. All of the combat groups, "coloured" or not, were socialist.

May Day roll calls in the bunkers or the ruins of demolished buildings. In unprecedented circumstances. They didn't only celebrate the holiday with speeches and listening to the May 1 broadcast from Moscow. They celebrated with special operations against the enemy.

A group from Mila went to Nalewki 47 in the middle of the day and lay in wait for a group of Germans, whom they defeated in a battle in the ruins. Stroop admitted his losses. The Jews returned to their base in the evening.

Not to mention groups from the brush shop on Franciskańska, as well as those from the Többens-Schultz block from Leszno 76 to Nowolipie 69. Stroop writes:

21 Dawn (trans.). 1st May was Workers' Day.

“245 Jews killed in battle or resisting. Encountered ringleaders and out-and-out bandits. In one case, a Jew who had been assigned to a transport that was supposed to be sent to a camp pulled out a hidden revolver and pumped several shots into a police lieutenant...The Jews captured today had, without exception, to be forcibly pulled from their bunkers. No cases of voluntary surrender today...We pulled a large number of Jews out of the sewers. In one case, German pioneers were laying down a bundle of explosives in order to blow up one of the sewer outlets. As soon as their backs were turned, a Jew snuck out, pulled the wick out of the bundle, took the explosives, and disappeared back into the sewer.”

This is how Jewish Warsaw celebrated its last May Day on the old streets.

The ghetto is in its death throes.

Buildings poke out of the rubble.

Burned out, blown up, cut apart.

Windows blown out by explosions, along with their frames. The streets dug up and ploughed by bombs, by cannonballs, by grenades...holes, pits, scattered piles of bricks...downed streetlights and telephone poles, broken furniture, rags, scrap metal lying everywhere.

But there was still life under the ground, ruthlessly repressed...Life...

The ruins looked on mutely through their blown-out windows at shapes that leap, that creep about the area, shuffling among the stones and mountains of bricks.

Jews once marched here in procession, with orchestras and banners... massive provisions...with Yiddish songs...The First of May.

And they are still walking now. They are here...The very last on the dying streets...The last incarnation of Jewish Warsaw...The First of May.

The struggle has entered a new stage. The penultimate.

XII

It was absolute hell.

The Inevitable was raging.

The fires, the murder.

Death peeked out everywhere.

From the ground, from the sky, from underground.

Stroop’s strategy was clear:

First, destroy everywhere above ground where Jews could shelter, hide,

The above-ground bunkers were all null and void

or take cover.

Most Jews were no longer on the surface, though. The greater part had been hiding in previously prepared underground shelters since the first day of the uprising. Those who stayed above ground were now being pushed downwards from their attics and apartments, or wherever else they might have been hiding. By bombs. By cannon fire. The above-ground bunkers were all null and void. Not everyone could get into the underground bunkers, though. Bunkers "broke down"; the number of homeless, "bunkerless" people was growing by the day.

Jews turned to the sewers now.

The third circle of Jewish defence: the underground sewer system. This was no good for Stroop. He had to drive the Jews back up, but had to do so from above.

The underground war began on the very first day. First with the attempt to drown those Jews who withdrew underground. He ordered the flow of water from all the sewers in the Jewish area to be shut off. The water backed up in the pipes. Stroop thought that by doing so, he could succeed in flooding all the cellars and bunkers with water. From one day to the next, he thought he would now be able to achieve his goal.

A Jewish fighter is caught and, below, another emerges from a bunker

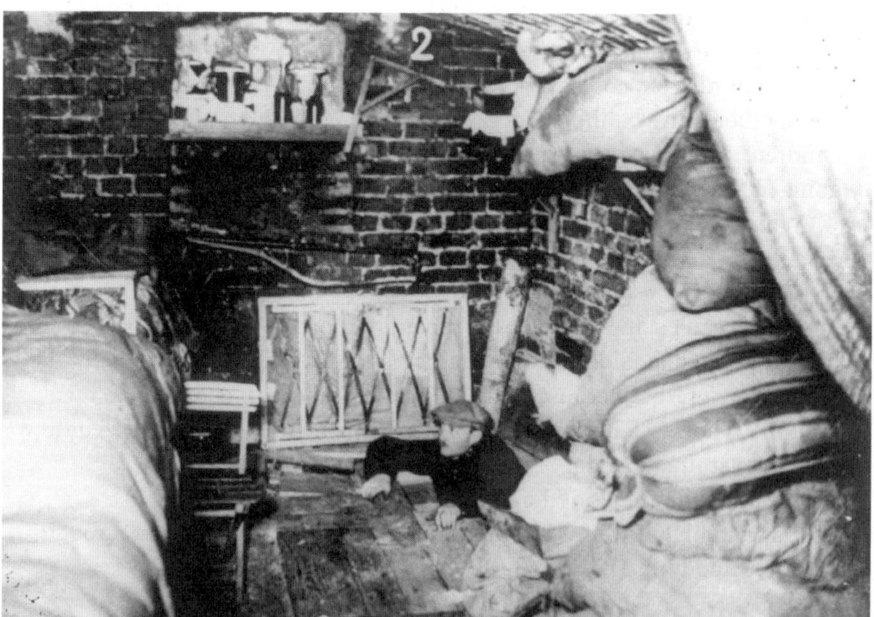

The planned atrocity did not come off.

It was technically difficult and was sabotaged to a degree by locals – Warsaw's Polish sewer workers. In his report the next day, Stroop wrote that the "water barrier" had been blown up by Jews. He was unable to obstruct the flow of water in the sewer system.

Stroop considered what to do. By ordering barrels of creosote to be poured into the sewers, he thought to turn the sewer water into a liquid caustic. This didn't work, either.

He sought another expedient against the Jews in the sewers and his next attempt at "chemical warfare" was more successful. Stroop called it *Nebelkerze*. Jews referred to it, more simply and more correctly, as "gas". The "candles" gave off a choking, burning, poisonous smoke. They spread panic and eventually became one of Stroop's main weapons against the Jews.

There were special *Aktionen* in the sewers every couple of days in which grenades and dynamite were also employed. Special reconnaissance groups, "SS men, bold, eager, ready to sacrifice themselves", climbed down into the sewer pipes to go hunting. They blew up the manholes on the Aryan side. In other places, they ordered the exits bricked over. They blocked the passageways with logs wrapped in barbed wire.

"By the first week, taking shelter in the sewers was already far from pleasant," said Stroop in his report.

And yet – the Jews weren't coming out.

Better the sewers than the Germans.

Vast hordes of people were wandering about down here as they had among the flames on the surface, entire families, with bundles, carrying children...A human wave rushing in one direction runs into another wave going in the other.

Which side is safer? Where is it dangerous? Where is there a leader to take these people from their adversity? It's dark – will they ever see daylight again?

People can't stand straight; the pipes are too low. They can't hold their heads up, their shoulders. The cloacal[22] water is rising – not because of the "water barrier," but because of the number of people. It comes up to their mouths. Whoever falls down is trampled. Anyone who loses his self-control might never find it again.

It was all the curses of the Torah.

Day and night, twenty-four hours a day, people were trudging through darkness and filth. They collapsed from weakness, hunger, and German

22 Sewer.

Chased by the flames... they start jumping

The blocks are now being systematically destroyed by fire. A well-guarded Stroop directs the destruction

stratagems. Anyone putting a hand in the water would pull out watches and wedding rings, carried down by the water from the hands of the dead, like pebbles from a stream...Would run across floating corpses. The murky water gurgles; it is coming back from somewhere.

"I had a report," Stroop writes one day, "of a large number of corpses floating in the main sewer underneath the ghetto, borne along by the current."

Did the current at least carry them as far as the Vistula? Did they come out after they died?

Stroop knew that there must still have been tens of thousands of Jews in the ghetto. He cannot see them and quickly arrives at the conclusion that he already knows from experience: the best and safest way to drag them out from underground is fire.

In the early days the fires were still localized, extinguished here and there. Less so afterwards. Only houses next to the wall were protected from fire – by Polish firefighters, their equipment at the ready, hoses full of water in their hands. They were strictly forbidden to let any water onto the Jewish side of the wall.

Their sole task was to make sure that the flames – like the Jews – be kept in their proper place.

New fires were lit in the ghetto every day.

"The blocks are now being systematically destroyed by fire," which was no longer extinguished. "Only then," writes Stroop, "do the Jews emerge from their bunkers and hideouts."

"The Jews have often stayed in the houses until the last possible minute, when the danger of being burned alive leads them to start jumping from the upper-storey windows onto mattresses, cushions, all kinds of bedding that they throw down first."

They jumped without mattresses and bedding, too.

Anything to keep out of German hands.

These were people who had neither weapons nor poison. Poles watched these scenes. They talked.

From houses by the wall that faced into the ghetto. Mass suicides. People in third, fourth, fifth storey windows, chased there by the flames. As well as those whom the flames embraced...Women carrying their children... Mothers running across the balconies...

How they scream and call for help...how they feel remorse. How they wrap the children in soft blankets to give them an easier death...How they throw them down...How they then jump themselves.

People watched this.

And shuddered in horror.

An episode from that time. A story told by Poles:

A fireman with a hose on the other side of the wall dividing the even side of the street from the odd. The fire is burning. He sees a mother and child on a fourth-floor balcony, the flames at their back. The woman is running across the balcony, from one end of the railing to the other. She can't make up her mind. She can't jump. The child is screaming, sticking its little hands out. She can't throw it down. The flames are coming closer and closer. In a minute, the hair on her young head will catch fire, her clothes will burn. She raises her burden, shows her child to the people on the other side of the wall. Or maybe she's lifting it up to God in heaven.

The firefighter cannot stand still. He can't hold his hand back. He lifts the hose, lets the water shoot upwards, and aims for the wall behind the image of Madonna and child among the flames...

The water comes closer. People are watching. The water doesn't reach the young woman's head.

A bullet to the neck. A German bullet. The water-jet drips downwards to the ground like a tear shed in vain.

A drop of pity.

It was a beautiful, warm spring that year. There was neither hail nor rain. No claps of thunder to let God's voice ring out against the wrong that one human being commits against another.

The cry of the murdered and burned climbed up to heaven. The anguish and fear of the mothers and children could not only rouse the pity of a god or an angel, but even that of a devil.

But sunbeams poured down from the sky, as if to increase the heat in the burning city; heaven didn't turn them into raindrops.

And the devil – the devil himself was in command of the German and Ukrainian SS men.

The Inevitable was raging.

The fires. The murder.

XIII

The post office of Warsaw's Jewish area was once located here, in the sprawling *Judenrat* building at Zamenhof 19, behind which was a large courtyard enclosed by an old wall. A little door in the wall led to another, even larger vacant lot. Several old trees provided shade.

An ideal spot for Stroop's executions.

One of his first orders on the first day of the *Aktion* was: "Kill them all!" Were Stroop to encounter a group of people pulled from a bunker on their way to the *Umschlagplatz,*[23] he would immediately take a "tithe" for himself. The square in front of the *Judenrat* was simultaneously a selection place. Stroop ordered his adjutants to carry out selections and he also did so himself. Some days, he picked Jews with red hair; others, men with full heads of hair, with Jewish noses, with "racial characteristics."

There was a constant sound of gunshots from the courtyard of Zamenhof 19. A rivulet of blood ran under the gate to the pavement, where it congealed in brownish-black heaps, like slabs of liver.

Stroop had to provide captured Jews to the labour camps at Trawniki and Poniatówa. From time to time, he'd also send a transport to T:II, the death camp at Treblinka. From May 12, he would send all the transports there, but sending people to die just isn't the same as killing them yourself.

The "functionaries" of Hitler's extermination machine always took a private pleasure in going beyond the call of duty in carrying out their "functions." Stroop was one of the bloodiest, one of the most frenzied. With time, he became one of occupied Europe's leading experts in pacification – burning habitations along with their inhabitants.

...Abundant death at every turn, masses of corpses – scattered alive under the blown-up buildings. Poisoning thousands of people in bunkers and sewers with gas. Looking on as people killed themselves by jumping from upper storeys. The sight of piles of bodies turned to carbon by the fires. The picture of corpses lying on the ground or "sitting" in doorways and courtyards, killed in their sleep by a stray bullet or shell fragment after they had collapsed, beyond exhaustion, onto the first place they could find, just so they could rest a while. A mother cradling a child in her arms, couples leaning on each other – in one last lean.

He himself took photos of this.

But looking didn't satisfy him, it wasn't enough for Stroop. He had to do the killing himself, up close, and look the victim in the eye.

Whenever he ran across a convoy of Jews, he had to stop and choose a couple to shoot. Once in a while, he would order a convoy to be exempted from selection: "Kill them all."

Stroop wouldn't let himself look at a Jewish face more than once. Two of the

23 The holding place at the station for deportees to the death camps

"most useful" and "most important" Jews, gravediggers, were like an arrow in his eye. He'd seen their faces a couple of times and was starting to recognize them. He couldn't stand it...After they had been shot, the remaining corpse gatherers, the twenty-five gravediggers, all disappeared the next day, absconding to the Aryan side through the cemetery.

The Germans who were there were put out by this; they needed these Jews. The corpse-clearers were to be kept alive longer than all the other Jews. They were supposed to be the last...

Now there was no one to clear away the bodies. Piles of bodies were rising in the *Judenrat* courtyard and all over the ghetto, fouling the air with their stench. Something had to be done right away.

Stroop came up with an idea.

He wanted to bring in a steamroller and have it *roll over the dead and iron them into the ground.*

He'd gone kill crazy.

He finally ordered the corpses to be thrown into the burning buildings to be incinerated.

There was one thing that the German witness who told of this couldn't bear:

The corpses were not searched for jewels or money...

Such things didn't happen later, when every captured Jew was searched more than thoroughly before being transported or shot. They were stripped naked, rectally probed. The women were given gynecological examinations.

To catch any "valuables".

That was the job of the witness who gave this testimony, to make sure that the Reich's treasury got what was coming to it.

At the same time, neither he nor other Germans forgot to look out for their own pockets, too...

Franz Konrad, chief of the *Werterfassung* in Warsaw, the second reporter and photographer of the Jewish revolt.[24]

A Konrad episode:

Jews who had been selected for shooting had to sit on the ground while waiting their turn. A boy and girl were sitting in one of the groups.

It was late. There were already stars in the sky.

The children were completely calm, resigned. They knew what was

24 Franz Konrad, chief of the Warsaw *Werterfassung* was arrested in Austria in 1946. There is a great deal of material about the Warsaw Ghetto in his written statement for the American Office of Investigations. His file also contains a collection of photographs from the Warsaw Ghetto uprising.

waiting for them. They could hear the constant salvoes from the *Judenrat* yard.

The girl spoke to the boy:

"See the stars up there? We'll be up there soon and no one will be able to hurt us anymore."

A fragment of a picture, a little detail...

The hell on the *Umschlagplatz* was no smaller and no different than in the earlier *Aktions* in Warsaw. No further description is needed.

XIV

The city of Warsaw fought three times during World War II, the second time behind the walls of the ghetto.

The Jews did not surrender.

As if the ghetto had taken over the struggle that Warsaw had lost – or broken off – in 1939.

After the terrifying bombardment of September 25 [1939] and the hurricane of shelling the day after; after the entire city, which had no more water to put out fires, had been set ablaze.

There was no chance of outside help.

A city completely surrounded by the enemy.

As if the Jews of Warsaw were now revising the earlier decision to surrender, to give up the struggle that was lost.

Now, as then, a civilian population that hindered – and helped – the soldiers in the fight.

A civilian population buffeted by danger and confusion.

From one bunker to the next. Out of the flames and into the fire. Groups running from one side in search of a way out bump into groups running in the opposite direction, thinking to save themselves in the place the others had fled...

In alleys between the burning buildings.

Even worse than 1939. Buildings were not only set alight by fire-bombs and flame throwers. Fires were being set up close.

Not to mention the incendiaries, bands of soldiers who shot bursts of bullets into the flames and hurled grenades to keep people from using the fires as cover for their escape.

Now as then, houses are being destroyed by bombs and artillery shells. Multitudes of people scattered beneath the ruins.

And worse.

Not only are explosives falling from above, but mines and other explosives are being laid up close. Detachments of sappers, led by engineers, carry out explosions expertly, blowing houses, cellars, bunkers up into the air.

People sit inside (they would like to live). Men, women, children, old people here and there, who still have not been killed.

And these here, the engineers, are visible in German photographs. They have laid their explosives as instructed, as if to blow up a bridge or quarry. They run off before the blast, take their places across from it, waiting, watching.

After the explosion – voices. The cries of the wounded, the terror-maddened. They run closer to – the German soldiers. Maybe they're thinking of helping these people, the victims of the catastrophe?

How could anyone think such a thing? It's just a sign that they're on the lookout for "the evicted" and "the smoked out", to make sure that no one gets away.

They have to get to them and drag them out as quickly as possible. To add more "heads" to the daily tally, to drag "valuables" out of their hole. They tore their clothes off, stripped them and robbed them of everything. Shot a few sometimes, sometimes shot them all.

Reinigung des Ghettobodens, they call it in German. Cleansing the ghetto area.

But the city behind the walls has still not capitulated, not even when Warsaw did so in 1939 and 1944.

Not even when death from German bullets looked like deliverance compared to this horror and pain...

When more than one person in the bunkers thought that dying in the gas chambers would be easier as long as you could breathe fresh air just once beforehand...

To breathe just once...

Oh, cruel, even crueler to themselves now than the Germans, these Warsaw Jewish martyrs of April and May 1943.

They sit choking in bunkers filled to bursting – they have to take in those who have been burned out. They can't strike a match or light a candle for lack of air. They endure temperatures of 40 and 50° C in the hideouts under the burning buildings. In the smoke and fumes, with no access to air. Someone is always fainting or dying. The others no longer have the strength to clear away the corpses.

People gasp, suffer, breathe their last – without a voice, without a word.

But they do not surrender.

Only in the evenings do they creep up to the surface – for air, for food, for news – each bit of which is more frightful than the one before. They no longer have the strength to cover their tracks, but they go back down and keep sitting.

They rarely leave the bunker – until the first German appears. Even then, someone still tries to shoot sometimes, if only to be able to say they resisted.

In certain places, people find last-minute strength when they hear banging or digging, when the Germans are approaching. They start to run. To run under the ground.

When they no longer have any tools, they use their fingernails...Dig. Dig. Crawl.

You can't tell what is more terrifying at that moment – their courage or their fear. The will to live or the resolve to die a death of one's own...

They snake along the raw earth on their naked bellies like moles, like worms. God!

O, you stiff-necked people, you stiff-necked people, how stubborn you were this time around!

Physically, though, they are defeated. Tear gas and *Nebelkerze*[25] finally drive them from the uncovered bunkers in a frenzy of coughing and sneezing. The executioners laugh.

And that wasn't quite everybody. There is always someone still hiding, concealed as if it were nothing, playing dead. There are very few instances of resignation now, of giving in to the inevitable.

There are, however, still suicides.

These are acts of resistance with knives, bricks, bare hands. Anything, rather than be taken alive.

Proclamations were issued. Manifestoes of dignity and revenge in the face of death.

They were defeated physically, but only rarely in spirit.

Fleeing the fires, leaping from upper storeys, they tried to drag their broken limbs through the streets and crawl into buildings where there were still no Germans.

Stroop later wrote: "We always noticed that when Jews running out of burning buildings caught sight of us, they ran back into the flames."

"You will all be sent to work," the German soldiers screamed. But the Jews didn't listen, didn't obey. Better the flames than the Germans.

...And they went back into the fire, like our ancestors who were strong enough to let themselves be burned at the stake rather than bow to superior strength or bend down to those they loathed.

25 Smoke grenades.

The victims and the smoked out...no one gets away

"One ought to read this bulletin from the front lines of fighting humanity's struggle so that our soldiers can be proud to be comrades-in-arms of those who are falling in the streets and houses of the fighting ghetto."

The words of an organ of the Polish underground.

...We, though, who belong to the people that produced this generation of fighters, we cherish our closeness, but not only to those who fought. We are also proud of those who had neither weapons nor a chance to fight, but showed their heroism in the way they acted during the defence.

Anyone who wants to understand this fight has to understand terror. Active Jewish resistance cannot be understood by anyone who has not first understood the passive.

XV

At first, the Germans estimated that the liquidation *Aktion* would take three days. The Polish underground gave the Jewish revolt two weeks. The two weeks were up on May 2. Stroop had already extended the deadline a couple of times, reassuring the Nazi General Gouvernement in Cracow that he would be done in another couple of days. But the third week of the *Aktion* had started, bringing with it only a new phase of the revolt.

Some streets had already been burned to the ground. The flames were starting to die down, the smoke had gradually settled, and the outline of what was happening, the nature of the new fight, was emerging more clearly, along with the ruins from the fire. Information was flying back and forth.

On May 1, Stroop announced that he was going to start sending out night patrols. The commander of the Jewish Combat Organization had reported on this as far back as April 23.

The Organization was finally able to engage with the enemy again without frequent contact. As long as the fires were still burning, the nocturnal Jewish reconnaissance detachments made all-too tempting a target, lit up as they were by the flames. But when the fires began to die down and certain neighbourhoods were once again dark, their chances improved a bit. Both sides had wrapped their boots in rags – the side that spotted the enemy and was the first to start shooting tended to be the side that won. It happened that the Germans didn't always know who they were looking at in the dark. The Jews were wearing German uniforms. A German helmet or pair of boots were like a prize for killing a German in the ruins on night patrol. But even better than that – guns. An automatic pistol and ammunition.

There was a serious shortage of ammunition. The Jews worried over every bullet. They saved the last couple for themselves.

On May 2, Krüger, the Senior SS and Police Commander, came down from Cracow for an inspection. Stroop had to present him with a more effective, more impressive piece of work. He chose the not completely burned down, not entirely liquidated block housing the two "armament firms", Transavia and Wiśniewski, that manufactured airplane parts. The block was at the edge of the ghetto, not far from the *Umschlagplatz*.

In his statement to the American investigators in Austria, Franz Konrad said:

> "A whole row of houses was set on fire in that area, leaving one of the buildings with no neighbours on any side. As *Obergruppenführer* Krüger and his escort were walking along the burning street with Stroop and his staff, a man approached with a report that Jews in the rear of the building were trying to escape from the fire through the attic windows on the roof...the whole group went into the courtyard and passed the evening hours watching the desperate acts of the

people illuminated by the flames. Some had already got onto the roof; the rest were trying to climb up from the windows via a narrow ledge...There was an order to shoot the people on the ledges. Anyone who didn't jump back from the window right away was killed by the bullets...The most terrible thing was the sight of children over three years old who also had the courage to escape to the narrow ledges of the roofs of the three- and four-storey buildings. They were shot down, too. Some of the wounded were snagged on open windows or balconies as they fell. Picture it: wounded people, a deep drop beneath them, a burning fire around them, growing closer...Those who were snagged and hanging in the air were not granted a bullet, just so their pain could go on...A real hunt was organized for the people on the roofs. Some tried to escape by leaping boldly into the abyss. It proved to be a death leap. In a panic, with the flames directly behind them, people were crammed together by the little window in the wall of fire. The Germans were shooting into the fire at whomever they could see. Anyone not felled by the bullets fell victim to the flames. These desperate people threw the dead out the windows to give themselves more room up there."

A close-up snapshot. A German account.
May 3, Stroop:
"1392 captured, 95 shot in combat, 19 bunkers blown up. Seized: rifles, pistols, homemade grenades. In most cases, the Jews offered resistance before leaving the bunkers with their guns in their hands. There were casualties...In some places, the Jews and bandits were firing pistols with both hands. Jewish women kept guns hidden in their panties...Only a large number of *Nebelkerze* induced the Jews to abandon their bunkers."

We know exactly who these obstinate Jews were.

This is the day when the big bunker at Franciskańska 30, on the same block as the Supply Section, was uncovered. It housed community and political activists, along with two writers,[26] and was one of the best-secured bunkers in the ghetto.

And those who were shooting and wounding Germans? We know them. They were what remained of the fighting groups from the brush shop on Świętojerska Street who had come over to Franciskańska on the third day of the uprising and made it their base. There are living witnesses to this fight, people who heard about it from those who were there and were later killed... This was one of the most heroic battles of the uprising. It went on for two

26 J.J. Proppes and Josef Kirman.

days in the ruins. A great many activists died in combat here. The survivors set up another base at Franciskańska 20 and 22, in the garbagemen's bunker.

The last bases of the Combat Organization – with the remnants of Warsaw's folksier Jews: porters, teamsters, "sluggers" – even former thieves.

The Combat Organization's last headquarters was the bunker of Yisroel-Isser, the king of the bums, at Mila 18.[27] Its last days were drawing near.

XVI

The *Aktion* went on.

The ghetto had already been transformed into a pile of smoking rubble. The fighters who defended bunker after bunker were growing fewer and fewer.

May 4:

A new *Aktion* on Leszno.

"As soon as the block of houses started burning, a fairly large number of Jews, driven out by smoke and flames, appeared as usual...They even tried to escape through the burning buildings. An unknown number of Jews who appeared on the roofs during the fire died in the conflagration. Others turned up on the upper floors at the very last minute and escaped a fiery death only by jumping..."

"188 Jews shot in the battle. Nocturnal clashes with Jewish patrols."

May 5:

"The Jews have mounted resistance in various locations...We were able to force our way into the bunkers only with the use of heavy explosives. Those within were annihilated..."

May 6, Stroop is amazed:

Contrary to all expectation, there were still people who had held up under the frightful, scorching heat living underneath the buildings of the Többens block at Leszno and Nowolipie that had been blown up two days earlier.

Stroop also describes a battle with Jews on the same day. They were firing large calibre pistols and throwing hand grenades. They wounded Germans. "356 Jews killed in battle," he noted.

Yes, it was strange – and not only for Stroop.

A moving, mysterious story.

A passage from Stroop's report for May 6:

"It appears that Jews who have escaped from the ghetto are coming back

27 Other sources also give the gangleader's name as Shmuel Osher (trans.)

with the intention of helping or liberating the ghetto Jews. A Jew who had escaped from Lublin was captured today in the vicinity of the ghetto wall. He was carrying a P.08 pistol,[28] two Polish hand grenades, and a considerable number of bullets..."

Who was this faithful fighter who broke back into the ghetto?

Will we ever learn more about him?

Stroop must once again extend the deadline for the end of the *Aktion*.

He writes continually of his amazement that the revolt has yet to be crushed completely.

Every couple of days, after a difficult fight in the ruins, he thinks that he has finally stumbled upon the activists' leaders – here, *khalutsim* and *khalutsot* (the terms he actually uses); the general staff of the PPR[29] there, as well as members of "the Jewish-Polish terrorist organization" that existed only in his head.

"These must be the people," he writes, "responsible for the fighting from day one. Their appearance, their weapons, their conduct all point to it."

A couple of days later, when the uprising has still not stopped, he writes the same thing about another group that fought to the death, shooting and wounding German soldiers and under no circumstances letting themselves be taken alive.

Stroop's description of the Combat Organization:

"There were groups," he writes in a general report, "comprised of from twenty to thirty young men between the ages of eighteen and twenty-five. They usually had a certain number of women with them, too. These groups were constantly provoking fresh acts of resistance.

"They had orders to defend themselves with weapons until the last minute and then kill themselves to avoid being captured."

In Stroop's "photo report" there are pictures inscribed:

"These bandits escaped by jumping before they could be captured."

It was true.

No members of the Combat Organization let themselves be taken alive.

Tracking down and killing the leaders of the revolt was a life-and-death matter for Stroop. Several times already, he had considered his wish fulfilled and announced that he knew where they were and was coming to get them – he's just caught one now. He turned out to be wrong every time.

But this time, he's making no mistakes.

In Stroop's report for May 7, we read:

28 i.e., a Luger Parabellum (trans.)

29 Polish Workers' Party (trans.)

"The location of the bunker of the inner party leadership is now known. It will be forced open tomorrow."

As often as we read these words, we still feel a twinge in our hearts. How can we warn them? We cannot warn them!

This time, alas, Stroop was not mistaken.

The saddest part was about to arrive. The inevitable.

XVII

The leaders of the Combat Organization had anticipated a great deal. A large part of its program had also been fulfilled.

Street assaults on the enemy's main forces by relatively large concentrations of fighters. The guerilla skirmishes of individual groups with smaller groups of Germans who found themselves cut off inside courtyards, between buildings, or among the ruins. Protecting the bunkers from discovery. The combat groups maintained order, tried to prevent mass panic during the fires, and in some cases supervised the evacuation of bunkers that were at risk. Tried, so far as possible, to alleviate the terrifying confusion.

The situation became more difficult by the day, the chances for fighting ever smaller. Firstly, because the ammunition was running out.

In his letter of April 23, the Organization's commander had already requested fresh deliveries. "Send long guns," he wrote. "We have no use for short ones..." After considerable effort, the Jewish representatives on the Aryan side indeed got a transport of guns, grenades, and ammunition from the *Gwardia Ludowa*,[30] but with the walls and sewers surrounded, there was no way of getting it into the ghetto. The only stores of ammunition belonged to private bunker watches, which had thus far taken no part in the fighting.

Fighting on without ammunition was starting to seem pointless to the Combat Organization. The moment they anticipated had arrived, the time to get the remaining activists out of the ghetto and onto the Aryan side. It had been agreed that when further combat became impossible, they would organize the withdrawal of their remaining forces from the ghetto. The survivors were to be taken out and sent to the partisans in the forests, where they could continue the struggle against the common enemy.

Those who had survived until now could say that their mission had been accomplished. They agreed to accept help from agents of the Polish underground.

The first such expedition to the Aryan side came to nothing. Four people

30 People's Guard (trans.)

set out in the sewers but didn't get through. One came back.

The next two messengers went out the same way a couple of days later. They made it to the Polish side.

They encountered difficulties. They stayed for more than a week until they managed to get everything ready, then returned the way they came – in the sewers.

When, after great difficulties, they finally got back to the ghetto, they were a day too late.

They went out on the night of May 8-9 and arrived in the ghetto on the ninth. The drama at Mila 18 had played out on May 8th.

After Mila 29, Mila 7, and Mila 9, the Combat Organization's last headquarters was Mila 18.

In a gigantic, lavishly armed and equipped bunker that belonged to a band of Jewish underworld types.

The fighters' reception in the bunker speaks to the people's love for the Combat Organization. Its popularity extended to the lowest elements, all the way to the underworld.

One of the surviving leaders tells the story:

> "A group from the Combat Organization stumbled into the bunker by chance, after which other fighting groups, about 300 people, found their way there, too. The leader of the gang welcomed them warmly. 'We're at your service,' said Yisroel-Isser. 'We'll be useful to you...'
>
> "And they really were helpful. They guided us by night and helped us observe the German positions by day. Later, after the ghetto had been completely burned down and it was almost impossible to recognize the streets, they were the only ones able to orient themselves...
>
> "Three weeks had passed since the fighting began. There was almost nothing left to fight with. The ammunition had run out. We were tormented by hunger. We were confronted with the prospect of a lingering death, but the feeling of having conscientiously fulfilled our mission, done our duty, comforted us. We didn't think about what was coming, because all that was coming was death. But when? And how?"

Connections with the Aryan side had all been sundered. Messengers who went out did not come back. A comrade brought news that there was a direct entry to the sewers at Franciskańska 20. There was also someone there who knew the way. The woman who wrote the memoir just quoted[31] took a group of people who needed to get out. They got to Franciskańska, met the comrades,

31 Zivia Lubetkin (trans.)

arranged the expedition, and came back to Mila 18 the following night with a couple of other comrades: “We were right there,” she writes, “and didn’t recognize it...Something had happened...No guards at the entrance...But the bunker has six entrances. We went to the second, the third, the fourth, but there was no guard anywhere. We were faint with apprehension. Suddenly we caught sight of shadowy figures moving around the next courtyard in the darkness. We took them for our people, out on nocturnal combat missions. We drew nearer. Yes, we recognized our comrades. They looked terrible, strange – mud-spattered, weak and trembling. One was faint, another had trouble breathing. One was wheezing. One of the women had head and leg wounds. They surrounded us. They told us what had happened.”

They told the story of the last act.

While they were lying down on the afternoon of May 8, the watch reported Germans approaching. They could hear their footsteps. In cases like this, the Jewish fighters employed one of two methods: either to go out with concealed weapons and suddenly open fire, giving some of their people a chance to escape, or else ignore German demands to come out and stay inside. The fighting would start when the enemy tried to break into the bunker. They could sometimes hold their position during the day – the Germans withdrew their main forces from the ghetto at night, so there was a chance to break through.

The fighters at Mila 18 knew that the Germans were using gas, but didn’t want to think about it...They decided to stay.

When the Germans broke the entrance open and started calling on the Jews to come out, the fighters stayed put.

Every exit from the bunker was surrounded.

“The Germans repeated their order. They promised that those who came out would be sent off to labour and threatened those who refused with death. The fighters responded by fortifying the entrance and getting ready to meet the Germans. The Germans made a second promise not to harm those who came out. The fighters did not respond.

“The Germans started to release gas. A terrible death drew near for the 120 fighters. There was no way out.

“The Germans released a little gas, then stopped right away. It was a matter of breaking the fighters’ spirit by carrying out a slow-motion execution.”

Then one of the comrades called out: “We’ll commit suicide. We won’t let them take us alive.”

And the comrades did as he said. One after the other. “If a revolver happened to jam, one comrade would ask another to give him the *coup de grâce*.”

Mordechai Anielewicz,
commander of the revolt:
I have been witness to the heroic battle of the Jewish fighters

Below:
Marek Edelman, Adas and Jan Kostanski. Kostanski – a teenage Gentile – smuggled food in and Jews out of the Ghetto and hid four members of the same family in a secret room at his home. After the revolt he cared for them underground for 105 days until liberated by Soviet soldiers

One young comrade used four bullets to kill his beloved mother before taking his own life. Another, who had been wounded a couple of days earlier, asked a colleague to shoot him...

The rest, those who didn't shoot themselves – there might not have been enough bullets – were suffocated by the gas...Only those comrades whom the fighters from Franciskańska met in the ruins recovered from the effects of the gas bomb, from Stroop's *Nebelkerze.*

Broken as they were, not a single one had gone out to the Germans.

Do you feel the power of these youths? The spiritual fortitude that was able to overcome the will to live, the fear of death?

In the cellar, in darkness, there was suffocating gas. Outside, there was air to breathe, a chance to live.

But they stayed true to their ideals. They did not go out to the enemy.

Mordechai Anielewicz, the commander of the revolt, died along with his army.

Fate willed it so.

So that the very brightest of all lights might shine around the young hero's head.

The halo of death.

XVIII

The night of May 8-9 was the decisive night for those who had survived. A second group of fighters experienced the same shock as the group from Franciskańska did among the ruins of the bunker at Mila 18. These fighters, who had gone out the night before to find an exit by way of Smocza Street, were fired on by a night patrol. They scattered across the ruins and only now, reduced in number, managed to get back to their base.

The base wasn't there anymore.

Around 2 a.m., the comrade from the expedition that had gone over to the Polish side to organize the withdrawal of the remaining activists climbed up out of the sewer entrance at Zamenhof and Stawki.

A second comrade stayed below with two Polish sewer-workers – their guides.

Franciskańska 30, Franciskańska 22, rows of apartment houses on Nalewki, Mila, Zamenhof – everything devastated, everything in ruins. No people, no traces. He went back to the sewer in despair, with the news that there was nobody left. Only on their way back did they encounter some of those who had stayed alive underground. They returned to the ghetto again.

A group was gathered together. A new run of long, hard hours in the

Zivia Lubetkin, the only woman on the High Command of ŻOB

Abrasha Blum continued to publish *Folkszajtung* (*The People's Gazette*) through the revolt

sewers. Only the next day, May 10, did the famous climb out of the sewer where Wronia and Prosta Streets meet take place.

Not everything went as arranged, but there was a truck waiting. A group of Jewish and Polish comrades guarded the street.

Dead tired, filthy with sewer-muck, in rags, but with guns in their hands, they came out of the sewer one at a time. Approximately forty people. Ready to spring into action at any minute. They jumped into the truck. In spite of the alerts, in spite of the pursuit, they crossed the bridge over the Vistula and got out of the city and onto the highway. They entered the forest that night near Wyszków. Hooked up with a detachment of partisans from the *Gwardia Ludowa.*

A second group of fighters, which took a different way out of the city, was not so lucky. They were caught in the village of Płudy, near Warsaw. Defended themselves to the last man, along with their heroic escort.

On the night of May 10, a group of twelve fighters from the Central Ghetto emerged from the sewer opening at the intersection of Łuckai and Prosta, and confronted the Germans on Grzybowska.

The fighters who had come out of the shop zone at an earlier date likewise survived only in part.

A total of eighty people, from all the groups in the Combat Organization,

Fighters Malka Zdrojewicz (right), Bluma Wyszogrodzka (centre) and Rukhele Lauschvits (?) who made grenades and Molotov-cocktails. Bluma was shot; Malka and Rachela were deported to camps. Malka survived and emigrated to Israel

escaped to the Aryan side.

Some of them fought as partisans in Polish formations, some took part in the general uprising in Warsaw in 1944 in their own detachment of the *Armia Ludowa.*

More and more victims fell – to battle, to denunciations, to disease. Only a very small group survived to be liberated.

Today [1948] there are no more than about ten members of the Warsaw Jewish Combat Organization living in Israel and Poland.

The same percentage as the general Jewish population in Poland.

XIX

The help provided by the *Gwardia Ludowa* in saving the surviving fighters was not the only act of fraternal solidarity on the part of the Polish underground organizations.

Contacts had been established much earlier.

The leaders of the Jewish Combat Organization had made every effort to win the support of the Polish underground movement for the Jewish preparations for the struggle.

First, with respect to weapons.

They turned to representatives of the government-in-exile and also sought to contact Polish military organizations.

In certain circles these Jewish efforts fell on deaf ears.

In spite of General Sikorski's attitude to the Jewish question and international political problems, there was no lack of fascist-reactionary and antisemitic elements in Polish political life who were happy about the "black work" that the Germans were doing on behalf of the Poles – "freeing Poland from the Jewish question."

As a result of the direct and indirect influence of these elements, the assistance of the delegates, though forthcoming, was half-hearted. If things were better in certain sectors, it was often due to the personal decency of a delegate of Poland's underground government.

The sector for putting Jews in touch with other countries was one such sector, among others.

At the time of the uprising, this lukewarm attitude to Jews on the part of certain members of the government-in-exile had the most decisive impact on the fate of the Jews.

They did nothing particularly effective about the weapon supply or anything else. They got by with compliments and acknowledgments of Jewish heroism. With articles in the underground press.

They took no energetic steps against even the lowest elements who made a living from denouncing, robbing, and persecuting Jews who were trying to stay alive on the Aryan side.

After lengthy and difficult efforts on the part of Jewish spokespeople, a proclamation was issued, threatening this scum with sanctions.

The call came too late.

This was one area in which the underground Polish government could have been of considerable help. Its authority in Poland was powerful enough by 1943 that it could have put a stop to the extortion gangs' persecution of

Fighters of the Polish underground man a barricade

Jews on the Aryan side.

This is just one more matter that yesterday's stretcher-bearers abandoned on the battlefield.

The attitude to Jews among the right-wing militia formations, which were concentrated in, or rather at the helm of the AKA,[32] was not much better. They held to the principle of standing at "parade rest", guns touching the ground, and they greeted the Jewish resolve to fight much as they did

32 The initials of the underground *Armia Krajowa* (Home Army).

Forces of the Polish underground amidst the ruins

the outbreak of the uprising – without much enthusiasm. At the start of the uprising, they advocated keeping it as brief as possible. They were afraid lest "the spark jump up" before the time was right.

The Jewish Organization found full camaraderie and support only among left-wing underground organizations and their military formations.

These organizations had no particularly great weapons capabilities. But they did whatever they could and put a quantity of guns and ammunition at the Jews' disposal both before and during the revolt.

The leader of the PPR gave a representative of the Combat Organization twenty-five rifles at the time of the uprising. A very great number, in view of their resources at the time.

The *Gwardia Ludowa* also organized a number of attacks on positions from which Germans were shooting into the ghetto.

On April 21, an unusually bold attack was launched on a machine-gun nest at Nowiniarska and Franciskańska that was raining bullets onto the ghetto.

The leader of the group that carried it out was a painter known as Jacek.

Stroop noted: "Two fatalities in the crew at the ghetto wall."

We find Stroop mentioning confrontations with armed Poles on other occasions, too, as, for instance, with the execution of thirty-five Poles captured at the edge of the ghetto with guns in their hands. Before their death, they are supposed to have called out, "Long live Poland! Long live Moscow!" which gives some indication of their ideological bent.

There were other cases of Poles helping the Jews with weapons – both then and later – not all of which have been publicized or discovered, just as we still do not know everything about Jewish acts of resistance.

The right-wing elements of the Polish underground were terrified lest the "Jewish spark" fly over the ghetto wall. The Germans were also afraid of this spark, but Göebbels' minions came up with a solution and got it ready on time.

First of all, the Katyn affair.

The atrocity was ready to happen then, once the German crime against the captured Polish officers had been pinned on Soviet forces.[33] The graves having been "found" a while earlier, the Germans were waiting to raise a hue and cry.

They did so on the first or second day of the *Aktion* in the ghetto. In newspapers and radio loudspeakers. The incident was masterfully exploited to divert the Poles' attention from what was happening in the ghetto.

So that they could present the *Aktion* against the Jews as a virtual act of vengeance for "the murder of Polish officers in Katyn."

The Germans in Warsaw never succeeded in sweet-talking the Poles and presenting themselves as their protectors. The Germans were roundly hated by Poles of every stripe, but when the names of the murdered officers were read out four times a day, with all their personal details, masses of people started to gather under the loudspeakers. Their attention was diverted from the ghetto. The feeling of protest against the ferocious German treatment of the wretched Jewish population, any interest or sympathy for their struggle, was weakened.

At the same time, the Germans wanted to show the Poles their iron fist through their cruelty to the Jews.

We find a clear indication of this in a couple of Stroop's notes about the impression made on the mood of the Polish population by his "hardness" towards the Jews.

Both he and Fischer, the governor, put up "informational" posters threatening death for sheltering Jews.

They encouraged the blue-uniformed Polish police to search out and capture Jews by promising them a third of whatever was taken.

This poison was effective.

Some were urged on with the tried-and-true old chestnut of "Judeo-Communism." The rest were terrorized.

Helped along by paid agents, the propaganda – overt and covert –

33 By 1990, even the Soviet government admitted that the massacre at Katyn was carried out by the NKVD (trans).

worked wonders.

As Easter approached, pictures of so-called atrocities committed by Soviet soldiers and commissars with Jewish noses appeared in display windows.

Reproductions of a Polish poster from 1920 depicting the Soviet menace in the form of a red devil were put up on the walls. The devil had a Jewish nose, too.

The message was always one and the same.

The Jew kills, robs, rapes women, drowns children. He controls governments and wants to devour the world.

It was just before Easter. Also, the Polish festival of spring. Warsaw watched a bizarre carnival entertainment.

A thick cloud of smoke was swirling over the north end of the city as if over a volcano. At night, the flames in which people were being burned alive could be seen. Men, women, and children were being murdered there, annihilated.

And here they were, making the Jew out to be the murderer, the killer of women and children.

There were idiots who believed it, believed that the guns the Jews were using to defend themselves were meant for the murder of Poles. That the Jews got them in Russian drops.

It was clear: the Germans were protecting the Polish population, liberating it from "the Jewish peril."

There weren't many of these idiots, but there were plenty of people eager to profit from the destruction of the Jews.

It was open season on Jewish lives and property.

The dregs of the underworld crawled up from the bottom and became the arbiters of the streets.

Taken aback by the protest against German crimes, by the horror of the murders and disgust with the miscreants among them, the best members of Polish society looked on at what was happening. Some left the city in terror. Others did what they could to help.

The mood of the disinterested masses changed from one day to the next, from astonishment to approval of what the Jews were doing, to satisfaction at seeing the Germans hurt. Then doubt crept in, mixing poison into their pity. In the end they went back to their own affairs, their day-to-day concerns. The Philistines returned to their egoism and indifference.

But the helpers did not give in. Not to fear, not to lies, not to hatred.

Risked their lives to save a wretched Jewish child, Jewish strangers, close friends.

Our brothers might have been lonely on the day of the final judgment, but they were not alone.

Along with members of various political parties, people who belonged to no party at all also offered the Jews a helping hand. Rich and poor, the most intellectually elite and simple members of the public. Their help and human feeling were a matter of heart.

There was a saying popular in intellectual circles that there was no decent person who didn't have a hand in helping Jews. Even "principled antisemites" were doing so.

Polish professors, artists, doctors, engineers, saved their colleagues in many cases.

Life being what it is, assimilated Jews with contacts among the Poles were the first to benefit from help of this kind. But they weren't the only ones.

This help assumed communal form in the activities of the Council to Help the Jews which, together with branches of the Jewish Co-ordinating Committee, the National Committee, and the representatives of various Jewish parties on the Aryan side, brought various forms of help to the Jews – sometimes on their own initiative.

Jews who had escaped the ghetto also received a certain amount of help from priests and nuns, people for whom helping the most unfortunate was a divine command.

Jewish and Polish blood were shed together at the edges of the ghetto.

So it was during the uprising. Collaboration and common struggle also took place later among the best of the Poles and Jews – it had been taking place all along.

In recalling the struggle and pain of the Jews, let us also recall the help of Poles who were fighting for the same ideal.

XX

Not every member of the Combat Organization to survive until May 9 made it out of the ghetto.

There were still three fighting groups that fought in the ghetto until the end.[34]

The end of Stroop's *Grossaktion*.

There were also unaffiliated fighters the whole time. The bunker guards,

34 Leaders of the three groups were Zacharia Artstein, Josef Farber and Yitskhok Blaustein.

the defenders who used to rise up just as the Germans were closing in on them.

There were those who froze at such times and failed to make use of their weapons. But there were others who poured all the wrath and defiance of innocents who have been sentenced to death into their last act. They modelled themselves after the "Party's" organized resistance.

Many people wanted to make their mark before dying.

Can you feel Humanity raising itself up to its full height after such debasing treatment?

Recapturing its dignity after so much degradation and devaluation?

It shouts the truth. It curses.

It spits square in the executioner's face. It has conquered its fear of death.

Individual and collective acts of defiance and revenge took place throughout the time of the struggle.

They assumed greater prominence in its final phase.

These two streams flowed into each other for the rest of the uprising.

The three remaining combat groups continued to make themselves heard in the echoes of a two-fold fire fight.

On May 9 and 10, Stroop notes continued resistance from uncovered bunkers. His detailed account of the combat groups emerging from the sewer on Prosta Street and his fruitless pursuit of them tallies with that of the Jews. Fifteen armed youths were captured in a tributary sewer immediately afterwards, and one more on the street. Stroop thinks that they, too, are members of the Combat Organization. The liquidation of the Jewish command structure so inspires him that he swears not to leave before the liquidation of the last Jew.

It is a goal that he never achieves.

But he still accomplished plenty...

The fighters' exit from the sewer bordering the Little Ghetto provoked particular anger in the executioner.

On May 12, he blew up and set fire to the Többens block on Prosta Street.

It turns out that there were Jews even there who did not let themselves be taken to Poniatówa, even though they were completely cut off from the Jews in the Central Ghetto, even though they had no Combat Organization groups. Their bitter and terrifying end was now at hand.[35]

May 13 was a day of great significance.

Everyone who was in Warsaw that day, even in the ghetto, remembers

35 The Little Ghetto was completely isolated from the other areas, which still had certain minimal opportunities for contact with one another.

the date, thanks to which we can shed some light on events that are mentioned in Stroop's report.

An incident that occurred while Jews were being dragged out of a bunker.

"A young girl who was supposed to be searched suddenly plucked a hand grenade from under her dress, pulled out the pin and tossed it into the midst of the men doing the searching. She herself jumped out of the way at lightning speed and hid among the ruins."

The story agrees in every detail with Jewish eyewitness testimony concerning a skirmish in the ruins of Franciskańska 20 and the girl who threw the grenade and died a hero's death.

We now know who that girl was. This incident took place on the day of the Soviet air strike on German targets in Warsaw.

A day that Jews remember well.

The air raid was an inspiration and a comfort to Jews in the ghetto and those on the Aryan side.

As at the time of the *Grossaktion* of August 1942, now, too, the Soviet air attack gave those about to be murdered a glimmer of hope in the jaws of death.

A fulfilment of their fever-dream of vengeance.

Confirmation of the expectation that a powerful protector might come to help the Jews. That the world would finally respond to the criminal injustice being done them.

But the response came only from the east. The western powers, which already controlled the airspace over the *Reich*, had the means to retaliate against the murder of the Jews.

They didn't take the trouble. They didn't have the will.

The efforts of Jews in those lands to move them towards it were vain.

The Germans' wall-guard suffered casualties in the air raid.

Jews tried to get out during the raid. Some of their attempts succeeded.

XXI

May 14:

The resistance is still not completely extinguished.

Nocturnal clashes between German patrols and "Jews firing pistols and sub-machine guns." The German watch was also being fired on from the Aryan side. Some were wounded. Stroop notes: "A skirmish with an armed group at the edge of the ghetto on the Aryan side.

"There were 10-14 men on roofs on the other side of the wall – we still don't know who they were. They wore German helmets and uniforms."

The Jews have developed a new habit, complains Stroop. They exploit the ruins, clambering up them to the higher floors, hiding in the intact remnants of attics, on burned-out staircases to which there is no longer any access. When they are uncovered – it happens often – they start throwing things down – grenades and Molotov cocktails, as they did in the early days." It turns out that just burning all the houses down was not enough to make it impossible for Jews to live in the ghetto.

Stroop is getting tired. He realizes that he's going to have to forget about fulfilling 100% of his mission. He's starting to talk about ending the *Aktion*.

At 3 p.m., *Nebelkerze* were dropped into 183 manholes at once, with the result that all the Jews still living in the sewers ran underground in the direction of the main sewer in the centre of the ghetto.

They were pulled out easily and liquidated, or else sent to the death camp of Treblinka II.

These wretched people, beleaguered already to the point of death, were deprived of a last chance to stay covered for a little while longer.

May 15:
Stroop's *Grossaktion* comes to an end.

Some of the twenty-nine bunkers uncovered that day were already uninhabited. Night patrols encountered only isolated Jews and were able to kill "no more" than nine. And yet today, too, he notes another group that defended itself with Molotov cocktails and hand grenades. The Germans found a time bomb with a detonator, ten kilos of explosive material, and a couple of pistols.

Every building in the cemetery was blown up and burned down on that day.

May 16, day 28 of the *Grossaktion*:
Stroop emphasized that only the main *Aktion* was over. For all the zeal with which he did his work, he did not fully accomplish his mission. He had to turn its continuation over to police battalion III/23. He sent for the commandant and, like any good boss, gave him precise instructions about what had to be done. His report provides an overview of the work still to come and the future of the ghetto area.

Also, a summary of all that was accomplished during the *Grossaktion*:

> 56,065 Jews captured or definitely killed, not including those who were killed but could not be counted. Stroop estimated their number at 5-

Jews being led to their deportation as the Ghetto burns

6000 souls.
Bunkers destroyed – 631
Weapons captured:
7 Polish rifles, 1 Russian, 1 German rifle. 56 pistols of various calibres, several hundred grenades, a couple of hundred Molotov cocktails. Also, explosive material, dynamite charges, a great deal of ammunition, some of it for automatics.
A lot of arms and ammunition stayed out of German hands because the warehouses in which they were stored blew up during the fires or getting to them in hiding places that had been gassed was impossible.[36]
Plunder:
108 horses, 1240 German uniforms, 600 pair military pants, a number of German helmets and other pieces of military equipment.
Money: 4,400,000 Polish zloty; 14,300 paper dollars, 9200 gold dollars, as well as a quantity of other foreign currencies. A great number of watches, rings, women's jewelry.
Excluding, of course, the money and gold dropped into the pockets of those who took part in this murderous looting.

Stroop emphasizes his achievements. Indeed, they got him an Iron Cross (his officers also received commendations).

"There was a Jewish quarter – it is no more." Not a single building in the area remained whole, other than the big Pawiak prison building on Dzielna St., which had been deliberately spared.

How characteristic...

The police battalion assumed the task of maintaining a constant pressure on those Jews still underground or in the ruins. They were to make sure that "they be deprived in every way of every possibility of existence."

Stroop ends with a suggestion:

The prison on Dzielna should be turned into a concentration camp. The prisoners should occupy themselves in collecting the millions of bricks, scrap iron and other raw materials that were supposed to be "shipped off for exploitation."

And this is the German total:

From thousands of buildings – mountains of old bricks.

From iron and other materials of service to humanity – heaps and piles of scrap, heaps of ash and trash.

From close to half a million living, productive human souls – ashes.

The German dream come true.

36 Stroop issued orders to poison food to prevent the Jews from 'reprovisioning' at night.

XXII

According to Stroop's report, the uprising lasted barely a month, but its last embers were not extinguished for weeks and weeks. The last echoes.

It was continued in the ruins.

The *Grossaktion* was over. The smaller one went on. Placards reading "*Halt! Stój!* Forbidden Zone" still hung from the walls around the ghetto. *Halt! Stój!* was written on the walls in chalk and in coal.

No one other than the Germans, their servants, and the prisoners who worked there was allowed into the ghetto right up until the very end.

The ruins were smoking and there was still some remaining life smouldering – along with the last, the very last remnant of the resistance.

Bunkers were still being uncovered, the last Jews in the ruins were trying to save themselves from death, to escape from the enemy's hands. People were still defending themselves with weapons.

The last fighters of the last combat groups left in the ghetto. News of them kept coming for more than a month.

New young people were joining them. The spirit of the organization lived on, even if life itself was flickering out.

They were still shooting – they were on their very last bullets – and still being shot at. The echoes spread through the ruins, through the whole of the city.

It sounds in our ears. It will resound in Jewish memory for generations.

Until death came to them, too, the very last. Their struggle came to an end with their ammunition.

From hunger and wounds, in clashes with the enemy, they keep falling away, one after the other.

With pistols tied to them by ropes (to prevent their being lost while climbing or jumping over ruins), devastated and hungry, these last fighters wandered about in the nights. They were looking for an exit from the sewers, just like those who had already got out. They had no luck. They came back empty every time.

There are no more masses of people running from death.

Those who go out at night now, looking for food, can't bear it because of the fear. Nobody sees anything, but a bit of tin that's come off a roof sounds odd. A window casement groans – it was swaying in the wind.

It was on such an evening that "Zachariasz" went out on a mission to find a way to get his boys out of the ghetto. He went to a street deep in no man's

From close to half a million living, productive human souls – ashes.
Soldiers of the Waffen SS in the last embers of the 'Great Action'

land.

He went and he vanished. Vanished forever among the ruins – the last ghetto commander.

They are all gone. But in underground holes, in the spaces between the mountains of bricks, in the untouched corners of burned-out buildings...

There were still signs of life there, flickering shadows.

But the last trail has still to come to an end. The real end of everything is not yet here.

Years later, witnesses spring up as if from the grave. They, too, have left this stage behind them. More and more new witnesses, people who held out there until September, into November and December, even one who didn't leave the ghetto until January 1944.[37]

Their stories are as strange as can be.

The end of the last bunkers, of people who fell into German hands so late. The emergence of gangs of informers, organized by the Germans with death threats, and robber bands – Jewish and Polish – an instance of degeneration in the precincts of this desolate land.

But there is a luminous last chapter, too. The "ruin groups", young people who live with the ideals of struggle and resistance. Also people who uphold the commandments of brotherhood and mutual self-sacrifice even in such circumstances.

The descriptions of this time, the experiences of these last Jews in the ghetto are stranger and more disconcerting than anything that the Jews had lived through before.

And even when this chapter finally reached its end – end of winter, spring, summer 1944 – explosions were constantly heard from the ghetto.

"It's nothing." People were reassuring each other. "They're blowing up buildings in the ghetto."

They tried to reassure themselves. To take heart. They knew that on Gęsia Street in the ghetto there was a concentration camp to which Poles were dragged off...there was talk of crematoria there, too.

Legends about the ghetto started to circulate. Mysterious stories, like tales from a far-off land.

There were Jews working in the ghetto now, too – new Jews from Bulgaria, Greece, the Balkans.

A Berlin firm called Meyer was granted a concession for "exploitation of the ghetto ruins." It was a business that paid.

Once again, they started blowing up all the buildings, dismantling the brickwork, shipping off the metal and scrap iron.

37 Yitzhak Zuckerman says that after the liberation, he spoke with a Jew who had held out in the ruins of the ghetto until the German withdrawal in 1945.

They laid a small branch railway line and filled the cars with freight.

They worked for over a year, "exploiting" and "leveling." The results can still be seen today.

They turned a vast settlement into a wasteland.

Let us swear on its sacred stones to be always with those who turn desert wastes into flourishing settlements. Not with those who hate and destroy, but with those love, who build and who sow.

XXIII

One late-winter day in 1944, a woman was walking from Bonifraterska St. to Inflancka, alongside the ghetto wall.

A Jewish woman living as a Pole.

Halt! Stój! Strefa Zakazana![38] The black inscriptions on the wall continued their warning. It was forbidden even to look inside.

It was as sad as can be.

There were no more tattered curtains fluttering in empty windows like cobwebs over fields of autumn harvest.

Since the third *Aktion*, there had been no windows in the ghetto at all.

People in striped uniforms with a star of David on the cap – Greek and Bulgarian Jews – were rummaging through bricks in places where Warsaw's Jews once lived.

There was only one lonely wall still standing in the rubble, like a ghost. The bricks scattered around it were a metre high. There was a man standing in the doorway of what had once been a balcony.

It looked out on the Woluwka market. There were women there with baskets of carrots and potatoes, and it was swarming with people buying and selling all kinds of things, mostly second-hand clothes and underwear.

A new spring was coming, a new summer. It was already late in the war.

The man in the doorway looked pensive. He looked at the people doing business nearby, at the free woman walking along the sidewalk. He was a prisoner in the hands of the devil – in a strange land with a strange language...

The sadness of the ghetto is in his eyes. He was as young, as handsome and as tragic as the boys and girls who fought here.

A young, foreign Jew among the ghetto ruins...

There are no Jews from Greece and Bulgaria in the ghetto wilderness today.

38 Forbidden zone (trans.)

People will soon be coming here – to build a new city. In the meantime, the scenery hasn't changed.

A whisper of thin grass covers the mountains of brick like the hair that keeps growing on a corpse.

A breeze blows over it.

Everywhere is quiet.

But whoever wanders there alone in the evening hears the echoes of voices...

A quorum of Jews holds services there every night. They are saying Kaddish for their people.

The melody of *El Moleh Rachamim* is carried on the wind.

A note has been incorporated in the melody, the sound of a shofar and a war horn.

Mordechai calling his troops to muster.

They come running from all sides, striding in the open air, through ghetto streets no longer there.

The executioner has fallen. The victim, too.

And the blood avenger is dead.

But he will rise again.

XXIV

Those of us who were in Warsaw then...

Our nostrils will always dream the smell of fire.

We will always see the pillar of smoke and fire that reached to heaven that spring. Will always hear explosions.

The explosions in Warsaw have still not stopped.

First came the continuation of the struggle. Then blowing up the buildings – no stone could be left resting on another. The transformation of the ghetto area into the landscape of a planet gone extinct.

We heard them every day, those explosions.

"They're blowing up the ghetto," people said...

Until the explosions increased again and grew stronger, blending into the gunfire of the general insurrection.

The gunfire of the Vistula front.

And six months later, the offensive barrage, the voice of liberation.

Only a handful of those who survived to get out of the ghetto lived to hear it...

And any Jew who comes to Warsaw should make a pilgrimage there first. To the place where the fires and the lives went out.

The cities that fought will be rebuilt

It is the desert that we crossed. With our own pillar of fire – the fight.

Fighting Warsaw set an example – like Leningrad, like Stalingrad.

There was a city within the city. Someone had already dubbed it Ghettograd.

For all its defeats and destruction, the city of Warsaw won a victory with its spirit – not just over the enemy, but also over those cities that remained intact.

That didn't raise a hand against superior strength, that bowed down to the all-powerful.

And the Jews who fought in Warsaw also set an example for their people.

For then and for now.

The cities that fought will be rebuilt.

And so will our people, which fought. Which fights on for its right to exist.

It will build itself up and be born anew – in struggle.

The fight is not yet done, not the Jews', not humanity's. It goes on.

The large-scale action was terminated at 2015 hours by blowing up the Warsaw Synagogue. The Great Synagogue, Tłomackie street. The synagogue was closed by the Germans in January 1940. By 1942, it was a warehouse for stolen furniture

A GRAVE MARKER

Their names:

Abraham, Isaac, Jacob.
Sarah, Rebecca, Rachel, Leah.
And a Reuben and a Simeon, a Joseph and a Benjamin.
A Moses and an Aaron, a Joshua.
And a Michael and a Raphael and a Gabriel.
And a David with a Solomon, a Saul, along with a Samuel.
And a Zechariah, an Ezekiel, even a Jeremiah.
And an Israel and an Enoch, a Tobias, a Menachem and a Simcha.
And a Meir and an Eliezer, a Hanina with a Jochanan – like the rabbis in the Mishna.
And a Tsvi-Hersh and a Dov-Ber, an Arye-Leib, a Wolf...
And a Miriam with a Deborah, a Hannah. A Ruth.
A Shoshana and a Penina.
And a Nekhe, a Temme, a Tsviye –
Like dear mothers of days gone by.
And a Frume – like a women's prayer leader.
And a Taybele, a Feygele – out of folksongs.

And because they were so young, still so close to their mothers' tender love, they gave each other childish names. And because they had grown up in Poland, they sometimes turned their Jewish names into Polish diminutives.

There was a Lutek and an Edek.
A Janek, a Mietek, a Sewek.
An Alek with a Tadek, and even a Staszek.
An Antek, a Marek, a Kazik.
And a Marysia and a Wandzia.
And a Stefa and a Rucia.

And those with a longstanding conspiratorial tradition behind them gave themselves serious underground names.

So there was Józef, one of the founders; a fighter called Ignaz, an Adam who spelled his name with Hebrew letters.

And there was an Andrzey, a Pawel, an Aleksander.

And there was a Michał and a Sigmund – among the most dedicated.

A Leon and an...Adolf...from Germany.

Yitzkhok 'Antek' Zuckerman (third from left) was Anielewicz's deputy in the Combat Organization. Second from left is Abraham Sutzkever, Holocaust poet and fighter; left is writer Shmerke Kaczerginski who survived the Vilna Ghetto

And those with a connection to the Land of Israel gave themselves names of pathos and greatness. Names from the desert, from the Bible.

And there was a Laban in another city, a member of the same party.

A Judah among the leaders, as among the Maccabees.

Not one, but two Mordechais, among the strongest and most ardent.

Let us sing the praises of these young people. Let us not mourn them. Let us love them as if they were all still here among us.

Let us keep them alive in us until our last breath.

The whole people could have been renewed in them.

They lived out the passions of an intense and stormy life in a single springtime.

Wove loves and friendships and wove them together – in a few months, in years cut short.

Nothing can compare with the glory of their fate.

Sombre, heroic, ecstatic – everything.

Yet as simple as a piece of black bread in the people's hand.

And they had the eyes of youth, some dreamy, some clever and lively.

And they had fair hair, like peasant boys; or black, curly hair like Gypsies. And any girl with blond hair grew it into long braids and went all over the country on missions.

And their lips were soft and puffy, half-childish yet. A breath of moisture on their cheeks, like early morning mist in the fields as spring is coming in.

A smile at the corners of their mouths, melancholy on their brows – what is more charming than the faces of the young?

Beautiful even in the face of death.

Unkempt, covered in filth, they lay in wait for the enemy, exhausted, their lashes reddened with smoke. Looked into the flames with their pupils dilated.

Those 18-20 and those 25 years old – blackened and grimy from the fight.

They were aglow. Eternity echoed in their steps.

They ran across the ledges of the buildings, dangled from ropes, rings, sheets – up and down.

Hard had no more meaning for them.

They hovered in the air over the Jewish roofs, like cherubs with their swords outstretched in their hands.

The whole nation could have been renewed in them.

Let no one dare take them from the mass of the people.

Let no one make a grab for their glory.

No family, no party, no country.

Let no one try to drag them down from the heights.

Let them go on floating over Jewish roofs as they did at that time.

Other peoples carve family names on monuments and memorial plaques. The names of martyrs, of fighters.

We are incapable of remembering – millions of surnames. Not even of those who fell in the fight.

There are those we know, and even more still nameless, unknown. We must not forget them.

There were those who prepared, who armed themselves to fight, who were killed before they lived long enough to fight. We must not forget them.

They were in Warsaw, in Cracow, in Vilna, in Bialystok, in Częstochowa, in Brody. In cities, villages, camps. Known and unknown. Those who resisted. And also those who were killed, who weren't able to last until the fight.

There are individual as well as communal acts which no witness lived to describe.

We must honour them all – the known, the unknown, the not-so-widely known, with the same love – all of them equally.

The monument to those who fell in the fight can only be a monument to the unknown soldier...

The memorial plaques are carved in the breasts of all the nation.

Their names:

Abraham, Isaac, Jacob.

Sarah, Rebecca, Rachel, Leah.

Josef, later Jürgen Stroop (centre) fought in the First World War. He joined the Nazi Party and SS in 1932, and was sent to Warsaw in April 1943 by SS leader Heinrich Himmler. He was awarded the Iron Cross 1st Class for his destruction of the Warsaw Ghetto.

The Stroop Report documents the suppression of the Jewish revolt. Bound in leather, it was a souvenir album for Heinrich Himmler to celebrate the victory, which took 20 days and 1,200 SS, Wehrmacht and police troops to accomplish.

The Report comprises a summary of operations, daily communiques and photographs. Three albums were prepared for Himmler, Krueger and Stroop; all were recovered and used as evidence at the Nuremberg trials as document No. 1061-PS

APPENDIX

The Stroop Report

TRANSLATION OF DOCUMENT NO. 1061-PS OFFICE OF CHIEF OF COUNSEL FOR WAR CRIMES.

THERE IS NO JEWISH GHETTO IN WARSAW ANYMORE

For the Fuehrer and their country the following fell in the battle for the destruction of Jews and bandits in the former ghetto of Warsaw:

(follows 15 names)

Furthermore: The Polish Police Sergeant Julian Zielinski, born 13 November 1891, 8th Commissariat fell on 19 April 1943 while fulfilling his duty.

They gave their utmost, their life, We shall never forget them. The following were wounded:

(follows the names of 60 Waffen SS personnel,

11 'Watchmen' from Training camps, probably Lithuanians, to judge by their names,

12 Security Police Officers in SS units

5 men of the Polish Police

2 regular Army personnel (engineers)

Units used in the action	Ave. no. of personnel used per day
SS Staff and Police Leader	6/5
Waffen SS	
SS_Panzer Grenadier Training and	4/0
Reserve Battalion 3,Warsaw	4/400
SS Cav. Training and Reserve Battalion	5/381

<u>Police</u>	
SS Police Regiment 22 I Bat.	3/94
III Bat.	3/134
Engineering Emergency Service	1/6
Polish Police	4/369
Polish Fire Brigade	166
<u>Security Police</u>	
Wehrmacht	
Light A-- Battery III/8 Warsaw	2/22
Engineers Det. Of Railway Armoured Trains	
Res.Bat Remoertow	2/42
Res.Eng.Bat. 14 Gora-Kalwaria	1/34
<u>Foreign Racial Watchmen</u>	
1 Lat "Trawniki" men	2/335
Total	36/2054

(Translator's note; this obviously means: 36 officers, 2054 men).

The creation of special areas to be inhabited by Jews, and the restriction of the Jews with regard to residence and trading is nothing new in the history of the East. Such measures were first taken far back in the Middle Ages; the could be observed as recently as during the last few centuries. These restrictions were imposed with the intention of protecting the Aryan population against the Jews.

Identical considerations led us as early as February, 1940 to conceive the project of creating a Jewish residential district in Warsaw. The initial intention was to establish as the Ghetto that part of the City of Warsaw which has the Vistula as its Eastern frontier. The particular situation prevailing in Warsaw seemed at first to frustrate this plan. It was moreover opposed by several authorities particularly by the City Administration. They pointed in particular that disturbances in industry and trade would ensue if a Ghetto were founded in Warsaw, and that it would be impossible to provide the Jews with food if they were assembled in a closed area.

At a conference held in March 1940, it was decided to postpone the plan of creating a Ghetto for the time being, owing to the above objections. At the same time a plan was considered to declare the District of Lublin the collecting area for all Jews within the Government General, especially for the evacuated or fugitive Jews arriving from the Reich. But as early as April 1940, the Higher SS and Police Leader, East, Cracow, issued a declaration that there was no intention of assembling the Jews within the Lublin District, In the meantime, the Jews had increasingly taken to crossing the frontier without permission and illegally. This was noted especially at the limits of the Districts of Lowicz and Skierniewice, conditions in the town of Lowicz became dangerous from the point of view of hygiene as well as from that of the Security Police, owing to these illegal migrations of Jews. The District President of Lowicz therefore, began to install Ghettos in his district in order to avoid these dangers.

The experiences in the district of Lowicz, after Ghettos had been installed, showed that this method is the only one suitable for dispelling the dangers which emanate repeatedly from the Jews.

The necessity of erecting a Ghetto in the city of Warsaw as well became more and more urgent in the summer in 1940, since more and more troops were being assembled in the district of Warsaw after the termination of the French campaign. At that time the Department for Hygiene urged the speedy erection of a Ghetto in the interest of preserving the health of the German forces and of the native population as well. The original plan of establishing the Ghetto in the suburb of Praga as intended in February 1940, would have taken at least 4 to 5 months, since almost 600,000 persons had to be moved. But since experience showed that greater outbreaks of epidemics might be expected in the winter months and since for this reason the District Medical Officer urged that the resettling action ought to be completed by 15 November 1940 at the latest, the plan of establishing a suburban ghetto in Praga was dropped; and instead, the area which hitherto had been used as a quarantine area for epidemics was selected for use as a Jewish residential area. In October 1940, the Governor ordered the Commissioner of the District President for the City of Warsaw to complete the resettlement necessary for establishing the Ghetto within the City of Warsaw by 15 November 1940.

The Ghetto thus established in Warsaw was inhabited by about 400,000 Jews. It contained 27,000 apartments with an average of 2.5 rooms each. It was separated from the rest of the city by partitions and other walls and by walling-up of thoroughfares, windows, doors, open spaces, etc.

It was administered by the Jewish Board of Elders, who received their instructions from the Commissioner for the Ghetto, who was immediately subordinated to the Governor. The Jews were granted self-administration on which the German supervising authorities intervened only where German interests were touched. In order to enable the Jewish Board of Elders to execute its orders, a Jewish Police force was set up, identified by special armbands and a special beret and armed with rubber truncheons. This Jewish Police force was charged with maintaining order and security within the Ghetto and was subordinated to the German and Polish Police.

II

It soon became clear, however, that not all dangers had been removed by this confining the Jews to one place. Security considerations required removing the Jews from the city of Warsaw altogether. The first large resettlement action took place in the period from 22 July to 3 October 1942. In this action 310,322 Jews were removed. In January 1943 a second resettlement action was carried out by which altogether 6,500 Jews were affected.

When the Reichsfuehrer SS visited Warsaw in January 1943 he ordered the SS and Police Leader for the District of Warsaw to transfer to Lublin the armament factories and other enterprises of military importance which were insulated within the Ghetto including their personnel and machines. The execution of this transfer order proved to be very difficult, since the managers as well as the Jews resisted in every possible way. The SS and police leader thereupon decided to enforce the transfer of the enterprises in a large scale action which he intended to carry out in three days. The necessary preparations had been taken by my predecessor, who also had given the order to start the large scale action. I myself arrived in Warsaw on 17 April 1943 and took over the command of the section on 19 April 1943, 0800 hours, the action itself having started the same day at 0600 hours.

Before the large-scale action began, the limits of the former Ghetto had been blocked by an external barricade in order to prevent the Jews from breaking out. This barricade was maintained from the start to the end of the action and was especially reinforced at night.

When we invaded the Ghetto for the first time, the Jews and the Polish bandits succeeded in repelling the participating units, including tanks and armoured cars, by a well-prepared concentration of fire. When I ordered a second attack, about 0600 hours, I distributed the units, separated from each other by indicated lines, and charged them with combing out the whole of the Ghetto, each unit for a certain part. Although firing commenced again, we now succeeded in combing out the blocks according to plan. The enemy was forced to retire from the roofs and elevated bases to the basements, dugouts and sewers. I ordered to construct [a barrier dam] below the Ghetto and filled with water, but the Jews frustrated this plan to a great extent by blowing up the turning off valves. Late the first day we encountered rather heavy resistance, but it was quickly broken by a special raiding party. In the course of further operations, we succeeded in expelling the Jews from their prepared resistance bases, sniper holes, and the like, and in occupying during the 20 and 21 April the greater part of the so-called remainder of the Ghetto to such a degree that the resistance continued within these blocks could no longer be called considerable.

The main Jewish battle group, mixed with Polish bandits, had already retired during the first and second day to the so called Muranowski Square. There, it was reinforced by a considerable number of Polish bandits. Its plan was to hold the Ghetto by every means in order to prevent us from invading it. The Jewish and Polish standards were hoisted at the top of a concrete building as a challenge to us. These two standards, however, were captured on the second day of the action by a special raiding party. SS Untersturmfuehrer Dohmke fell in this skirmish with the bandits; he was holding in his hand a hand grenade which was hit by the enemy and exploded, injuring him fatally. After only a few days I realized that the original plan had no prospect of success, unless the armament factories and other enterprises of military importance distributed throughout the Ghetto were dissolved. It was therefore necessary to approach these firms and to give them appropriate time for being evacuated and immediately transferred. Thus, one of these firms after the other was dealt with, and we very soon deprived the Jews and bandits of their chance to take refuge time and again in these enterprises which were under the supervision of the Armed Forces. In order to decide how much time was necessary to evacuate these enterprises thorough inspections were necessary. The conditions discovered there are indescribable. I cannot imagine a greater chaos than in the Ghetto of Warsaw. The Jews had control of everything, from the chemical substances used in manufacturing explosives to clothing and equipment for the Armed Forces. The managers knew so little of their own shops that the Jews were in a position to produce inside these shops, arms of every kind, especially hand grenades, Molotov cocktails, and the like.

Moreover, the Jews had succeeded in fortifying some of these factories as centers of resistance. Such a center of resistance in an Army accommodation office had to be attacked as early as the second day of the action by an Engineers Unit equipped with flame-throwers and by artillery. The Jews were so firmly established in this shop that it proved to be impossible to induce them to leave it voluntarily; I therefore resolved to destroy this shop the next day by fire.

The managers of these enterprises, which were generally also supervised by an officer of the Armed Forces, could in most cases make no specified statements on their stocks and the whereabouts of these stocks. The statements which they made on the number of Jews employed by them were in every case incorrect. Over and over again we discovered that these labyrinths of edifices belonging to the armament concerns as residential blocks, contained rich Jews who had succeeded in finding accommodations for themselves and their families under the name of "armament workers" and were leading marvelous lives there. Despite all our orders to the managers to make the Jews leave those enterprises, we found out in several cases that managers simply concealed the Jews by shutting them in, because they expected that the action would be finished within a few days and that they then would be able to continue working with the remaining Jews. According to the statement of arrested Jews, women also seem to have played a prominent part. The Jews are said to have endeavoured to keep up good relations with officers and men of the armed forces. Carousing is said to have been frequent, during the course of which business deals are said to have been concluded between Jews and Germans.

The number of Jews forcibly taken out of the buildings and arrested was relatively small during the first few days. It transpired that the Jews had taken to hiding in the sewers and in especially erected dugouts. Whereas we had assumed during the first days that there were only scattered dugouts, we learned in the course of the large-scale action that the whole Ghetto was systematically equipped with cellars, dugouts, and passages. In every case these passages and dugouts were connected with the sewer system. Thus, the Jews were able to maintain undisturbed subterranean traffic. They also used this sewer network for escaping subterraneously into the Aryan part of the City of Warsaw. Continuously, we received reports of attempts of Jews to escape through the sewer holes. While pretending to build air-raid shelters they had been erecting dugouts within the former Ghetto ever since the autumn of 1942. These were intended to conceal every Jew during the new evacuation action, which they had expected for quite a time, and to enable them to resist the invaders in a concerted action. Through posters, handbills, and whisper propaganda, the communistic resistance movement actually brought it about that the Jews entered the dugouts as soon as the new large-scale operation started. How far their precautions went can be seen with the fact that many of the dugouts had been skillfully equipped with furnishing sufficient for entire families, washing and bathing facilities, toilets, arms and munition supplies, and food supplies sufficient for several months. There were differently equipped dugouts for rich and for poor Jews. To discover the individual dugouts was difficult for the units, as they had been efficiently camouflaged. In many cases, it was possible only through betrayal on the part of the Jews.

When only a few days had passed, it became apparent that the Jews no longer had any intention to resettle voluntarily, but were determined to resist evacuation with all their force and by using all the weapons at their disposal. So-called battle groups had been formed by Polish-Bolshevists: they were armed and paid any price asked for available arms.

During the large-scale action we succeeded in catching some Jews who had already been evacuated and resettled in Lublin or Treblinka, but had broken out from there and returned to the Ghetto, equipped with arms and ammunition. Time and again Polish bandits found refuge in the Ghetto and remained there undisturbed, since we had no forces at our disposal to comb out this maze. Whereas it had been possible during the first days to catch considerable numbers of Jews, who are cowards by nature, it became more and more difficult during the second half of the action to capture the bandits and Jews. Over and over again new battle groups consisting of 20 to 30 or more Jewish fellows, 18 to 25 years of age, accompanied by a corresponding number of women kindled new resistance. These battle groups were under orders to put up armed resistance to the last and if necessary to escape arrest by committing suicide. One such battle group succeeded in mounting a truck by ascending from a sewer in the so-called Prosta and in escaping with it (about 30 to 35 bandits). One bandit who had arrived with this truck exploded 2 hand grenades, which was the agreed signal for the bandits waiting in the sewer to climb out of it. The bandits and Jews – there were Polish bandits among these gangs armed with carbines, small arms, and in one case a light machine gun – mounted the truck and drove away in an unknown direction. The last member of this gang, who was on guard in the sewer and detailed to close the lid of the sewer hole, was captured. It was he who gave the above information. The search for the truck was unfortunately without result.

During this armed resistance the women belonging to the battle groups were equipped the same as the men: some were members of the Chalutzim* movement. Not infrequently, these women fired pistols with both hands. It happened time and again that these women had pistols or hand grenades (Polish "pineapple" hand grenades) concealed in their bloomers up to the last moment to use against the men of the Waffen SS, Police, or Wehrmacht.

The resistance put up by the Jews and bandits could be broken only by relentlessly using all our force and energy by day and night. <u>On 23 April 1943 the Reichs Fuehrer SS issued through the Higher SS and Police Fuehrer East at Cracow his order to complete the combing out of the Warsaw Ghetto with the greatest severity and relentless tenacity</u>. I therefore decided to destroy the entire Jewish residential area by setting every block on fire, including the blocks' residential buildings near the armament works. One concern after the other was systematically evacuated and subsequently destroyed by fire. The Jews then emerged from their hiding places and dugouts in almost every case. Not infrequently, the Jews stayed in the burning buildings until, because of the heat and the fear of being burned alive they preferred to jump down from the upper stories after having thrown mattresses and other upholstered articles into the street from the burning buildings. With their bones broken, they still tried to crawl across the street into blocks of buildings which had not yet been set on fire or were only partly in flames. Some of the Jews changed their hiding places during the night, by moving into the ruins of burnt out buildings, taking refuge there until they were found by our patrols. Their stay in the sewers also ceased to be pleasant after the first week. Frequently from the street, we could hear loud voices coming through the sewer shafts. Then the men of the Waffen SS the Police or the Wehrmacht Engineers courageously climbed down the shafts to bring out the Jews and not infrequently they then stumbled over Jews already dead, or were shot at. It was always necessary to use smoke candles to drive out the Jews. Thus, one day we opened 163 sewer entrance holes and at a fixed time lowered candles into them, with the result that the bandits fled from what they believed to be gas to the center of the former Ghetto, where they could then be pulled out of the sewer holes there. A great number of Jews, who could not be counted, were exterminated by blowing up sewers and dugouts.

The longer the resistance lasted, the tougher the men of the Waffen SS, Police and Wehrmacht became; they fulfilled their duty indefatigably in faithful comradeship and stood together as models and examples of soldiers. Their duty hours often lasted from early morning until late at night. At night search patrols with rags wound round their feet remained at the heels of the Jews and gave them no respite. Not infrequently they caught and killed Jews who used the night hours for supplementing their stores from abandoned dugouts and for contacting neighbouring groups or exchanging news with them.

Considering that the greater part of the men of the Waffen-SS had only been trained for three to four weeks before being assigned to this action, high credit should be given for the pluck, courage, and devotion to duty which they showed. It must be stated that the Wehrmacht Engineers, too, executed the blowing up of dugouts, sewers, and concrete buildings with indefatigability and great devotion to duty. Officers and men of the Police, a large part of whom had already been at the front, again, excelled by their dashing spirit.

Only through the continuous and untiring work of all involved did we succeed in catching a total of 56,065 Jews whose extermination can be proved. To this should be added the number of Jews who lost their lives in explosions or fires but whose numbers could not be ascertained.

During the large-scale operation the Aryan population was informed by posters that it was strictly forbidden to enter the former Jewish Ghetto and that anybody caught within the former Ghetto without a valid pass would be shot. At the same time these posters informed the Aryan population again that the death penalty would be imposed on anybody who intentionally gave refuge to a Jew, especially lodged, supported, or concealed a Jew outside the Jewish residential area.

Permission was granted to the Polish police to pay to any Polish Policeman who arrested a Jew within the Aryan part of Warsaw one third of the cash in the Jew's possession. This measure has already produced results.

The Polish population for the most part approved the measures taken against the Jews. Shortly before the end of the large-scale operation, the Governor issued for special proclamation and which he submitted to the undersigned for approval before publication to the Polish population; in it he informed them of the reasons for destroying the former Jewish Ghetto by mentioning the assassinations carried out lately in the Warsaw area and the mass graves found in Katyn; at the same time they were asked to assist us in our fight against Communist agents and Jews.

The large-scale action was terminated on 16 May 1943 with the blowing up of the Warsaw Synagogue at 2015 hours.

Now, there are no more factories in the former Ghetto. All the goods, raw materials, and machines there have been moved and stored somewhere else. All buildings etc. have been destroyed. The only exception is the so-called Dzielna Prison of the Security Police, which was exempted from destruction.

III

Although the large-scale operation has been completed, we have to reckon with the possibility that a few Jews are still living in the ruins of the former Ghetto; therefore, this area must be firmly shut off from the Aryan residential area and be guarded. Police Battalion 111/23 has been charged with this duty. This Police Battalion has instructions to watch the former Ghetto, particularly to prevent anybody from entering the former Ghetto, and to shoot immediately anybody found inside the Ghetto without authority. The Commander of the Police Battalion will continue to receive further direct orders from the SS and Police Fuehrer. In this way, it should be possible to keep the small remainder of Jews there, if any, under constant pressure and to exterminate them eventually. The remaining Jews and bandits must be deprived of any chance of survival by destroying all remaining buildings and refuges and cutting off the water supply.

It is proposed to change the Dzielna Prison into a concentration camp and to use the inmates to remove, collect and hand over for re-use the millions of bricks, the scrap-iron, and other materials.

IV

Of the total 56,065 Jews caught, about 7000 were exterminated within the former Ghetto in the course of the large-scale action, and 6,929 by transporting them to T.II, which means 14,000 Jews exterminated altogether. Beyond the number of 56,065 Jews an estimated number of 5 to 6,000 were killed by explosions or in fires.

The number of destroyed dugouts amounts to 631.

Booty:
7 Polish rifles, 1 Russian rifle, 1 German rifle,
59 Pistols of various calibres,
several hundred hand grenades, including Polish and home-made ones,
several hundred incendiary bottles,
home-made explosives,
informal machines with fuses,
a large amount of explosives, ammunition for weapons of all calibres, including some machine gun ammunition.

Regarding the booty of arms, it must be taken into consideration that the arms themselves could in most cases not be captured, as the bandits and Jews before being arrested, threw them into hiding places or holes which could not be ascertained or discovered. The smoking out of the dugouts also often made the search for arms impossible. As the dugouts had to be blown up at once, a search later on was out of the question.

The captured hand grenades, ammunition, and incendiary bottles were at once re-used by us against the bandits.

Further booty:
1,240 used military tunics (part of them with medal-ribbons Iron Cross and East medals)
600 pairs of used trousers,
other equipment and German steel-helmets.
108 horses, 4 of them still in the former Ghetto (hearse)

Up to 23 May 1943 we had counted:
4.4 million Zloty;
furthermore about 5 to 6 million Zloty not yet counted,
a great amount of foreign currency, e.g. 814,300 in paper and 89,200 in gold, moreover valuables (rings, chains, watches etc.) in great quantities.

State of the Ghetto at the termination of the large-scale operation:

Apart from 8 buildings (Police Barracks, hospital, and accommodations for working-parties) the former Ghetto is completely destroyed. Only the dividing walls are left standing where no explosions were carried out. But the ruins still contain a vast amount of stones and scrap material which could be used.

Warsaw, 16 May 1943.
The SS and Police Fuehrer in the District of Warsaw
SS Brigadefuehrer and Majorgeneral of Police

Daily Reports

Copy
SS Services Teletype Message
From the SS and Police Fuehrer in the District Of Warsaw
Ref. No. I ab St/Gr 16 07 Re: Ghetto Operation
To: The Higher SS and Police Fuehrer East Cracow
Warsaw, 20 April 1943
Journal No. 516/43 secret

Progress of Ghetto Operation on 19 April 1943:
Closing of Ghetto commenced 0300 hrs. At 0600 order to Waffen SS (strength: 16/850) to comb out the remainder of the Ghetto. Hardly had the units fallen in, strong concerted fire-concentration by the Jews and bandits. The tank used in this action and the two heavy armoured cars pelted with Molotov cocktails (incendiary bottles). Tank twice set on fire. Owing to this enemy counterattack, we had at first to take the units back. Losses in first attack: 12 men (6 SS-men, 6 Trawniki-men).

About 8.00 hrs. second attack by the units, under the command of the undersigned. Although the counterattack was repeated, this time we succeeded in combing out the blocks of buildings according to plan. We caused the enemy to retire from the roofs and elevated prepared positions into the cellars or dugouts and sewers. During this combing-out we caught only about 200 Jews. Immediately afterwards raiding parties ware directed to dugouts known to us with the order to pull out the Jews and to destroy the dugouts. About 300 Jews captured. We found out that the Jews had taken to the sewers. Sewers were completely inundated, to make staying there impossible. About 1730 hrs. we encountered very strong resistance from one block of buildings including machine gun fire. A special raiding party invaded that block and defeated the enemy, but could not catch the resistors. The Jews and criminals resisted from base to base, and escaped at the last moment across lofts or through subterranean passages. About 2030 hrs. the external barricade was re-enforced. All units were withdrawn from the Ghetto and dismissed to their barracks. Re-enforcement of the barricade by 250 Waffen-SS men. Continuation of operation on 20 April 1943.

Units at my disposal:

SS-Panzer-Gren. Res.Batl	6/400

SS-Cav. Res. Batl.	10/450
Police	6/165
Security Service	2/40
Trawniki-men	1/150
Wehrmacht:	
1 10-cm-Howitzer	1/7
1 Flame-thrower	1
Engineers	2/16
Medical detachment	1/1
3 2.2-cm A.A. guns	2/24
1 French tank of the Waffen-SS	
2 heavy armoured cars of the Waffen-SS	
Total:	31/1262

I put Major of Police Sternagel in command of today's operations subject to my further instructions if necessary.

At 0700 hrs. 9 raiding parties were formed, each 1/36 strong, consisting of mixed units, to comb out and to search the remainder of the Ghetto intensively. This search is still in progress; its first objective will be completed by 1100 hrs. In the meantime it has been ascertained that part of the Ghetto which is no longer inhabited but not yet released and which contains several armament factories and the like, there were several centers of resistance, which were so strong that the tank could not go through. 2 raiding parties defeated these centers of resistance and made a passage for the tank men. In this operation we already had two wounded (Waffen-SS).

Enemy is much more cautious than yesterday, since he has of course learned of the heavy arms at our disposal.

My intention is first to comb out completely the remainder of the Ghetto and then to scan out in the same manner the so-called uninhabited Ghetto, which so far has not been released. It has been ascertained in the meantime that the latter part of the Ghetto contains at least 10 to 12 dugouts, some of which are even in armament factories. The whole operation is made more difficult because there are still factories in the Ghetto which must be protected against bombardment and fire, because they contain machines and tools.
A further report will follow tonight.

The SS and Police Fuehrer in the District of Warsaw
Signed: Stroop
SS-Brigadefuehrer and Majorgeneral of Police
Certified copy: SS-Sturmbannfuehrer

Copy Teletype message
From the SS and Police Fuehrer in the District of Warsaw
Warsaw, 20 April 1943.
Ref. No. I ab St/Gr 16 07-Journal No. 517/43 secret
Re: Ghetto Operation
To the Higher SS and Police Fuehrer East
SS-Obergruppenfuehrer and General of Police
Krueger - or deputy
Cracow

Supplementing my teletype message of 20 April 1943 - Ref. St/Gr 16 07 Re: Ghetto operation – I beg to report as follows:

The resistance centers ascertained within the uninhabited but not yet released part of the Ghetto were crushed by a battle group of the Wehrmacht-Engineers and flame-throwers. The Wehrmacht had one wounded in this operation, shot through the lungs. Nine raiding parties broke through as far as the northern limit of the Ghetto. 9 dugouts were found, their inmates crushed when they resisted, and the dugouts blown up. What losses the enemy suffered cannot be ascertained accurately. Altogether the 9 raiding parties caught 505 Jews today: those among them who are able-bodied were kept ready for transport to Poniotow. At about 1500 hrs. I managed to arrange that the block of buildings occupied by the Army Accommodation Office said to be occupied by 4000 Jews is to be evacuated at once. The German manager was asked to call upon the Jewish workers to leave the block voluntarily. Only 28 Jews obeyed this order. Thereupon I resolved either to evacuate the block by force or to blow it up. The A.A Artillery-3 2-cm. guns used for this operation had two men killed. The 10-cm howitzer, which also was used, expelled the gangs from their strong fortifications and also inflicted losses on them, as far as we were able to ascertain. This action had to be broken off owing to be fall of darkness. On 21 April 1943 we shall attack this resistance center again, as far as possible it will remain blocked off during the night.

In today's action we caught, apart from the Jews reported above, considerable stores of incendiary bottles, hand grenades, ammunition, military tunics, and equipment.

Losses: 2 dead (Wehrmacht)

7 wounded (6 Waffen SS, 1 Trawniki-man)

In one case the bandits had laid pressure mines. I have succeeded in causing the firms W.C. Toebbens, Schultz and Co., and Hoffmann to be ready for evacuation with their entire personnel on 21 April 1943 at 0600hrs. In this way, I hope to get the way free at last for cleaning out the Ghetto. The Trustee Toebbens has pledged himself to induce the Jews, numbering about 4 to 5,000, to follow him voluntarily to the assembling point for being resettled. In case this has as little success as was attained in the case of the Army Accommodation Office, I am going to clean out this part of the Ghetto as well by force. I beg to acknowledge receipt of the order which the Obergruppenfuehrer communicated to me by telephone today, and of the powers granted to me.

Next report on 21 April 1943 at noon.

The SS and Police Fuehrer in the District of Warsaw
signed: Stroop
SS-Brigadefuehrer and Majorgeneral of Police
Certified copy: SS-Sturmbannfuehrer

Copy Teletype Message
From: The SS and Police Fuehrer in the District of Warsaw
Warsaw, 21 April 1943.
Ref. No. I ab St/Gr 16 07 Journal No. 527/43
Re: Ghetto Operation
To The Higher SS and Police Fuehrer East
SS-Obergruppenfuehrer and General of Police
Krueger - or deputy
<u>Cracow</u>

Progress of Ghetto Operation on 21 April 1943:
Supplementing the report which I made today about 1400 hrs. by telephone, I beg to report:
Forces at my disposal as of 20 April 1943.
Start of Operation: 0700 hrs. the whole of the Ghetto has continued to be cordoned off since the start of the operations on 19 April 1943.

Inasmuch as the special operation concerning the block of buildings occupied by the Army Accommodation Office had to be interrupted yesterday because of darkness, one battle group reinforced by Engineers and heavy artillery was again sent into the block of buildings, which was found to contain an enormous quantity of dugouts and subterranean passages firing from time to time. I resolved therefore to blow up these passages which we had discovered and subsequently to set the entire block on fire. Not until the building was well aflame did screaming Jews make their appearance, and they were evacuated at once. We had no losses in this operation. Precautionary measures were taken in order to ensure that the conflagration remained localized.

The main body of our forces was detailed to cleanse the so-called uninhabited, but not yet released, part of the Ghetto by proceeding from South to North. Before we started this action, we caught 5,200 Jews who had been employed in enterprises under the supervision of the Commissioner for Armament (Rue Ko-Betrieben) and transported them under armed guard to the Railway Station) which had been chosen for use in the resettlement. I formed 3 search-parties to which were attached special raiding parties who had the duty to attack or blow up the dugouts which were known to us. This operation had to be interrupted when darkness set in, after one half of the area mentioned had been combed out.

Continued on 22 April 1943, 0700 hrs.

Apart from the Jews who were to be evacuated, 150 Jews or bandits were killed in battle and about 80 bandits were killed when their dugouts were blown up. The enemy today used the same arms as on the previous day, particularly home-made explosives. Samples have been kept by the SS and Police Fuehrer. For the first time we observed the participation of members of the Jewish Women's Battle Association (Chalutzim Movement). We captured rifles, pistols, hand grenades, explosives, horses, and parts of SS uniforms.

Own loses: 2 Policemen, 2 SS men, 1 Trawniki man. (light wounds)

The SS and Police Fuehrer in the District of Warsaw
Signed: Stroop
SS-Brigadefuehrer and Majorgeneral of Police
Certified copy: SS-Sturmbannfuehrer

Copy Teletype message
From the SS and Police Fuehrer in the District of Warsaw
Warsaw, 22 April 1943.
Ref: No. I ab St/Gr 16 07 - Journal No. 530/43 secret.
Re: Ghetto Operation.
Supplement to Par. 1 of letter of 21
April 1943.
To: The higher SS and Police Fuehrer of Police
Krueger - or deputy
Cracow

Our setting the block on fire achieved the result in the course of the night that those Jews whom we had not been able to find despite all our search operations left their hide-outs under the roofs, in the cellars, and elsewhere, and appeared at the outside of the buildings, trying to escape the flames. Masses of them – entire families – were already aflame and jumped from the windows or endeavoured to let themselves down by means of sheets tied together or the like. Steps had been taken so that these Jews as well as the remaining ones were liquidated at once. During the whole night there were shots from buildings which were supposed to be evacuated. We had no losses in our cordoning forces. 5,300 Jews were caught for the evacuation and removed.

The SS and Police Fuehrer in the District of Warsaw
signed: Stroop
SS-Brigadefuehrer
and Majorgeneral of Police
Certified copy: SS-Sturmbannfuehrer

Copy Teletype Message
From the SS and Police Fuehrer in the District of Warsaw
Warsaw, 22 April 1943.
Ref. No. I ab St/Gr 16 07 - Journal No. 531/43 secret. Re:
Ghetto Operation
To: The Higher SS and Police Fuehrer East
SS-Obergruppenfuehrer and General of Police
Krueger - or deputy
Cracow

Progress of the Ghetto Operation on 22 April 1943 up to 1200 hrs:
One raiding party was dispatched to invade once more the block of buildings which for the greater part had burned out or was still aflame, in order to catch those Jews who were still inside. When shooting again started from one block, against the men of the Waffen-SS, this block also was set on fire, with the result that a considerable number of bandits were scared from their hide-outs and shot while trying to escape. Apart from those, we caught about 180 Jews in the yards of the buildings. The main body of our units continued the cleansing action from the line where we terminated this action yesterday. This operation is still in progress. As on the proceeding days local resistance was broken and the dugouts we discovered were blown up. Unfortunately there is no way of preventing part of the Jews and bandits from taking refuge in the sewers below the Ghetto, where we can hardly catch them since they have stopped the flooding. The City Administration is not in a position to frustrate this nuisance. Neither did the use of smoke candles or the introduction of Creosote into the water have the desired result. Cooperation with the Wehrmacht splendid.

The SS and Police Fuehrer in the District of Warsaw
signed: Stroop
SS-Brigadefuehrer and Majorgeneral of Police
Certified copy: SS-Sturmbannfuehrer

Copy Teletype Message
From the SS and Police Fuehrer in the District of Warsaw
Warsaw, 22 April 1943.
Ref. No. ab St/Gr-16 07 -Journal No. 532/43 secret
Re: Ghetto Operation.
The Higher SS and Police Fuehrer East
SS-Obergruppenfuehrer and General of Police
Krueger - or deputy
Cracow

Progress of operation of 22 April 1943. Report on action up to 1200 hrs. has already been submitted by my message of today. Continuing, I beg to report:

Then the special raiding party searched the remainder of the blocks as already reported, they met with resistance at some places; they had the following success: 1,100 Jews caught for evacuation, 203 bandits and Jews killed, 15 dugouts blown up. They captured 80 incendiary bottles and other booty.

Units at my disposal: as reported by teletype message on 21 April 1943. Journal No. 516/43 secret.

Our losses: SS-Untersturmfuehrer Dehmke (dead); enemy hit a hand grenade which he carried. (SS-Cav.Res.Batl.)

1 Sergeant of Police (shot through the lungs)

When the Engineers blew up the dugouts, a considerable number of Jews and bandits were buried under the ruins. In a number of cases it was found necessary to start fires in order to smoke the gangs out.

I must add that since yesterday some of the units have been shot at time and again from outside the Ghetto, that is, from the Aryan part of Warsaw. Raiding parties at once entered the area in question and in one case succeeded in capturing 35 Polish bandits, Communists, who were liquidated at once. Today it happened repeatedly when we found it necessary to execute some bandits, that they collapsed shouting ‘Long live Poland’, ‘Long live Moscow’.

The operation will be continued on 23 April 1943, 0700 hrs.

The SS and Police Fuehrer in the District of Warsaw
signed: Stroop
SS-Brigadefuehrer and Maj.Gen. of Police
Certified copy: SS-Sturmbannfuehrer

Copy   Teletype Message
From the SS and Police Fuehrer in the District of Warsaw
Warsaw, 23 April 1943.
Ref. No.: I ab St/Gr-16 07-Journal No. 538/43 secret
Re: Ghetto Operation
To: The Higher SS and Police Fuehrer East
SS Obergruppenfuehrer and General of Police
Krueger - or deputy
Cracow

Progress of Ghetto Operation on 23 April 1943:
Start: 700 hours.
The whole of the former Ghetto had been divided for the purposes of today's combing-out operations into 24 districts. One reinforced searching party was detailed to each district with special orders. These assignments had to be carried out by 1600 hours.

Result of this action: 600 Jews and bandits ferreted out and captured, about 200 Jews and bandits killed, 48 dugouts, some of them of a quite elaborate character, blown up. 70 captured apart from valuables and money - some gas masks.

The units had been informed that we intended to terminate the operation today. In the morning the Jews had already become aware of this instruction. This is why a renewed search by the searching parties was undertaken after an interval of 1 to 1 1/2 hours. The result was, as always, that again Jews and bandits were discovered to be in various blocks. From one block shots were even fired against the cordoning units. An attack by a special battle group was ordered and in order to smoke the bandits out, every building was now set on fire. The Jews and bandits held out, every building was now set on fire.

The Jews and bandits held their fire up to the last moment and then concerted their fire against the units. They even used carbines. A number of bandits who were shooting from balconies were hit by our men and crashed down. Furthermore, today we discovered a place said to have been the headquarters of the "PPR"; we found it unoccupied and destroyed it. It was on this 5th day of operations that obviously we found the worst of the terrorists and activists, who so far had always found ways and means to dodge every searching or evacuation action.

A racial German reported that again some Jews had escaped through the sewers into the Aryan part of the city. We learned from a traitor that there were some Jews in a certain house.

A special motorized raiding party invaded the building and caught 3 Jews,

2 of them females. During this operation their motorcar was pelted with one incendiary bottle and one explosive; 2 Policemen were wounded.

The whole operation is rendered more difficult by the cunning way in which the Jews and bandits act; for instance, we discover that the hearses which were used to collect the corpses lying around at the same time bring living Jews to the Jewish cemetery, and thus they are enabled to escape, from the Ghetto. Now this way of escape also is barred by continuous control of the hearses.

At the termination of today's operation about 2200 hours, we discovered that again about 30 bandits had passed into a so-called armaments factory, where they had found refuge. Since the forces are storing goods of great value in this enterprise, this factory was requested to evacuate the building by noon on 24 April: This will enable us to cleanse that labyrinth of a building tomorrow.

Today 3,500 Jews were caught who are to be evacuated from the factories. A total of 19,450 of the Jews have been caught for resettlement or already evacuated. Of these about 2,500 Jews are still to be loaded.

The next train will start on 24 April 1943.

Strength as of 22 April 1943, without 150 Trawniki men; these have already been put at the disposal of the Eastern Command as reinforcement for another assignment.

Our losses:

2 Police corporals ("SB") wounded
1 Trawniki man wounded.

The operation will be continued on 24 April 1943, 1000 hours. This hour was chosen so that Jews who may still be in the Ghetto will believe that the operation was actually terminated today.

signed: Stroop
SS-Brigadefuehrer and Majorgeneral of Police
Certified copy: SS-Sturmbannfuehrer

Copy Teletype message
From: The SS and Police Fuehrer in the District of Warsaw
Warsaw, 24 April 1943.
Ref. No.: I ab St/Wdt-16 07 Journal No. 545/43 secret.
Rc: Ghetto operation.
The Higher SS and Police Fuehrer East
SS Obergruppenfuehrer and General of the Police
Krueger - or deputy
Cracow

Progress of operation on 24 Aril 1943, start 1000 hours:
Contrary to the preceding days, the 24 searching parties which had again been formed did not start at one end of the Ghetto, but proceeded from all sides at the same time.

Apparently, the Jews still in the Ghetto were deceived by the fact that the operation did not start until 1000 hours into believing that the action really had been terminated yesterday. The search action, therefore, had especially satisfactory results today. This success is furthermore due to the fact that the non-commissioned officers and men have meanwhile become accustomed to the cunning fighting, methods and tricks used by the Jews and bandits and that they have acquired great skill in tracking down the dugouts which are found in such great number. The raiding parties having returned, we shot about to clean a certain block of buildings, situated in the north-eastern part of the former Ghetto. In this labyrinth of buildings there was a so-called armaments firm which reportedly had goods worth millions for manufacture and storage. I had notified the 'Wehrmacht' of my intentions on 23 April 1943 about 2100 hours and had requested them to remove their goods by 1200 hours, Since the Wehrmacht did not start this evacuation until 1000 hours, I felt obliged to extend the term until 1800 hours. At 1815 hours a search party entered the premises, the building having been cordoned off, and found that a great number of Jews were within the building. Since some of these Jews resisted, I ordered the building to be set on fire. Not until all the buildings along the street and the back premises on either side were well aflame did the Jews, some of them on fire, emerge from these blocks, some of them endeavoured to save their life by jumping into the street from windows and balconies, after having thrown down beds, blankets, and the like, Over and over again we observed that Jews and bandits, despite the danger of being burned alive, preferred to return into the flames rather than risk being caught by us. Over and over again the Jews kept up their firing almost to the end of the action: thus, the engineers had to be protected by a machine gun when toward nightfall they had to enter forcibly a concrete building which had been very strongly fortified. Termination of today's operation; on 25 April 1943 at 0145 hours, 1660 Jews were caught for evacuation, 1814 pulled out of dugouts, about 330 shot. Innumerable Jews were destroyed by the flames or perished when the dugouts were blown up. 26 dugouts were blown up and an amount of paper money, especially dollars was captured; this money has not yet been counted.

Our forces; as on the preceding day, minus 50 men of the Waffen-SS. Our losses: 2 SS-men and one Trawniki man wounded.

Altogether there have now been caught in this action 25,500 Jews who lived in the former Ghetto. Since there are only vague estimates available of the actual number of inhabitants I assume that now only very small numbers of Jews and bandits still remain within the Ghetto.

Operation will be continued on 25 April 1943, 1300 hours.

I beg to acknowledge receipt of teletype messages nos. 1222 and 1223 of 24 April 1943. As far as can be predicted, the present large-scale operation will last until Easter Monday inclusive.

Today large posters were affixed to the walls surrounding the Ghetto, announcing that everybody who enters the former Ghetto without being able to prove his identity will be shot.

The SS and Police Fuehrer in the District of Warsaw
Signed: Stroop
SS Brigadefuehrer and Major General of Police.
Certified Copy: SS Sturmbannfuehrer

Copy Teletype message
From: The SS and Police Fuehrer in the District of Warsaw
Warsaw, 25 April 1943.
Ref. No. I ab/Wdt-16 07 - Journal No. 549/4 secret.
Re: Ghetto operation.
To: The Higher SS and Police Fuehrer East
SS Obergruppenfuehrer and General of Police
Krueger - or deputy
Cracow

Progress of operation on 25 April 1943, start 1300 hours:
For today 7 search parties were formed, strength 1/70 each, each allotted to a certain block of buildings.

Their order was: 'Every building is to be combed out once more; dugouts have to be discovered and blown up, and the Jews have to be caught. If any resistance is encountered or if dugouts cannot be reached, the buildings are to be burnt down.' Apart from the operations undertaken by these 7 search parties, a special operation was undertaken against a centre of bandits, situated outside the wall surrounding the former Ghetto and inhabited exclusively by Poles.

Today's operation of the search parties ended almost everywhere in the starting of enormous conflagrations. In this manner the Jews were forced to leave their hide-outs refuges. A total of 1,960 Jews were caught alive. The Jews informed us that among them there are certain parachutists who were dropped here and bandits who had been equipped with arms from some unknown source. 274 Jews were killed.

As in the preceding days, uncounted Jews were buried in blown up dugouts and, as can be observed time and again, burned with this bag of Jews today. We have, in my opinion, caught a very considerable part of the bandits and lowest elements of the Ghetto. Intervening darkness prevented immediate liquidation. I am going to try to obtain a train for T II tomorrow. Otherwise liquidation will be carried out tomorrow. Today also, some armed resistance was encountered; in a dugout three pistols and some explosives were captured. Furthermore, considerable amounts of paper money, foreign currency, gold coins and jewelry were seized today.

The Jews still have considerable property. While last night a glare of fire could be seen above the former Ghetto, today one can observe a giant sea of flames. Since we continue to discover great numbers of Jews whenever we search and comb out, the operation will be continued on 26 April 1943. Start: 1000 hours.

Including today, a total of 27,464 Jews of the former Warsaw Ghetto, have been captured.

Our force; as on the previous day.
Our losses; 3 members of the Waffen-SS
and one member of the security police wounded.

Total losses up to date:

	wounded
Waffen SS	27
Police	9
Security Police	4
Wehrmacht	1
Trawniki men	9
	50

	and 5 dead
Waffen SS	2
Wehrmacht	2
Trawniki men	1
	5

The SS and Police Fuehrer in the District of Warsaw,
Signed: Stroop
SS Brigadefuehrer and Majorgeneral of Police
Certified copy SS Sturmbannfuehrer

Copy Teletype message
From: The SS and Police Fuehrer in the District of Warsaw
Warsaw, 26 April 1943.
Ref.No. I. ab-St/Wdt-16 07 -Journal No. 550/43 secret
Re: Ghetto operation - supplementary report
To: The Higher SS and Police Fuehrer East
SS-Obergruppenfuehrer and
General of Police Krueger - or deputy
Cracow

1) The operation on 25 April 1943, was terminated at 2200 hrs.
2) General effects of the execution of this operation.
The Poles resident in Warsaw are much impressed by the toughness of our operations in the former Ghetto. As can be seen from the daily reports, the general situation has greatly calmed down since the beginning of that operation within the city area of Warsaw. From this fact one may conclude that the bandits and saboteurs resided in the former Ghetto, and that now all of them have been destroyed.

In this connection the fact may be of some interest, that an illegal ammunition store was seen to explode when we burned down a certain building in the dwelling area on which we were working at the time.

The SS and Police Fuehrer in the District of Warsaw
signed: Stroop
SS Brigadefuehrer and Majorgeneral of Police

Certified copy: SS-Sturmbannfuehrer

Copy Teletype Message
From: The SS and Police Fuehrer in the District of Warsaw
Warsaw 26. April 1943
Re: No. I ab-St/Wdt-16 07 Journal No. 551/43 secret.
To: The Higher SS and Police Fuehrer East
SS-Obergruppenfuehrer and General of Police
Krueger - or deputy
Cracow

Start of operation: 1000 hrs.
The whole of the former Ghetto was once more combed through today by the same search parties, each of them allotted to the same district as before. In this way I tried to bring about that the leaders of those parties work in thoroughfares, blocks of buildings, and courtyards which they know already and that thus they are able to penetrate deeper and deeper into the maze of dugouts and subterranean passages. Almost every search party reported resistance, which however they broke either by returning fire or by blowing up the dugouts.

It becomes clearer and clearer that it is now the turn of the toughest and strongest among the Jews and bandits. Several times dugouts have been forcibly broken open, the inmates of which had not come to the surface during the whole of this operation. In a number of cases the inmates of the dugouts were hardly in a condition when the dugout had been blown up, to crawl to the surface. The captured Jews report that many of the inmates of the dugouts became insane from the heat, the smoke, and the explosions. Several Jews were arrested who had kept close liaison with the group of Polish terrorists and collaborated with it. Outside the former Ghetto we arrested 29 Jews. During today's operation several blocks of buildings were burned down. This is the only and final method which forces this trash and sub-humanity to the surface. We again captured arms, incendiary bottles, explosive charges and considerable amounts of cash and foreign currency. Today I also arranged that several so-called armament and defence enterprises will evacuate their stores from the building at once, so that these buildings in which the Jews now have taken refuge, under the protection of the army of the German Wehrmacht and police, can be combed out. In one case we again discovered, as previously, that in a building which had been said to contain a giant enterprise there existed in fact almost no stores or goods. One factory was closed without further ado, and the Jews were evacuated.

Result of today's operation:

30 Jews evacuated, 1,330 Jews pulled out of dugouts and immediately destroyed, 362 Jews killed in battle. Caught today altogether: 1,722 Jews. This brings the total of Jews caught to 29,186. Moreover, it is very probable that numerous Jews have perished in the 13 dugouts blown up today and in the conflagrations. At the time of writing not one of the Jews caught still remains within Warsaw. The scheduled transport to T II had no success. [Note of translator: This probably means that no Jews were available for regular transport to the extermination camp.]

Strength: as on preceding day.
Our losses: none
End of today's operation at 2145 hrs.;
will be continued on 27 April 1943 at 0900 hrs.
The SS and Police-Fuehrer in the District of Warsaw
signed: Stroop
SS Brigadefuehrer and Major-General of Police
Certified copy: SS-Sturmbannfuehrer

Copy Teletype Message
From: The SS and Police Fuehrer in the District of Warsaw
Warsaw, 27 April 1943.
Ref. No. I ab-St/Gr 16 07 Journal No. 555/43 secret
Re: Ghetto Operation
To The Higher SS and Police Fuehrer East
SS-Obergruppenfuehrer and General of Police
Krueger - or deputy
Cracow

Progress of operation on 27 April 1943. Start: 0900 hrs:
For today's operation I formed 24 raiding parties with the same task as on several days of last week; they had to search the former Ghetto in smaller groups. These search parties pulled 780 Jews out of dugouts and shot 115 Jews who resisted. This operation was terminated about 1500 hrs.; some of the parties had to continue to operate because they had found more dugouts.

At 1600 hrs. a special battle group, 320 officers and men strong, started cleansing a large block of buildings situated on both sides of the so-called Niska street in the North-Eastern part of the former Ghetto. After the search the entire block was set on fire, after having been completely cordoned off. In this action a considerable number of Jews were caught. As before, they remained in the dugouts, which were either below the ground or in the lofts of the building until the end. They fired their arms to the last moment and then jumped down into the street, sometimes from as far up as the fourth floor, having previously thrown down beds, mattresses, etc. but not until the flames made any other escape impossible.

A total of 2,560 Jews were caught today within the former Ghetto, of them 547 were shot. Moreover, Jews in a not ascertainable number perished when dugouts were blown up or in the flames. The sum total of Jews formerly residing in the Ghetto caught in this action now count to 31,746.

We learned from an anonymous letter that there were a considerable number of Jews in a block of buildings adjoining the North-Eastern part of the Ghetto, but outside of it. A special raiding party under the command of lst.Lt. of police DICHL was dispatched to attack these buildings. The raiding party discovered a gang of about 120 men, strongly armed with pistols, rifles, hand grenades, and light machine guns, who resisted. They succeeded in destroying 24 bandits in battle and arresting 52 bandits. The remainder could not be caught or destroyed, since darkness intervened. The buildings, however, were surrounded at once so that an escape will hardly be possible. This cleansing action will be continued tomorrow. Moreover we arrested 17

Poles, among them 2 Polish Policemen who should have been aware, among other things, of the existence of this gang. In this operation we captured 3 rifles, 12 pistols, partly of heavier calibre, 100 Polish 'pineapple' hand grenades, 27 German steel helmets, quite a number of German uniforms, tunics and coats which even furnished with the ribbon of the East medal, some reserve magazines for machine guns, 300 rounds of ammunition etc. The leader of the raiding party had a difficult task because the bandits were disguised in German uniform. But despite this fact, he did his duty with great efficiency. Among the bandits who were caught or killed, there were some Polish terrorists who were identified with certainty. Today we succeeded furthermore in discovering and liquidating one of the founders and leaders of the Jewish-Polish resistance movement. The external appearance of the Jews whom we were catching now shows that it is now the turn of those Jews who were the leaders of the entire resistance movement. They jumped from the burning windows and balconies, abusing Germany and the Fuehrer and cursing the German soldiers.

SS-men who descended into the sewers discovered that a great number of corpses of perished Jews are being washed away by the water.

Cordoning Forces

Our strength: From 0700 to 1900 hrs	288 German police
	200 Trawnikimen
	140 Polish Police
From 1900 to 0700 hrs	288 German Police
	250 Waffen-SS
	140 Polish Police
Strength in the operation:	3/115 German Police
	4/400 Waffen-SS
	1/6 Engineering Serv.
	2/30 security police
	2/21 Engineers

Our losses: 3 wounded,: 2 Waffen-SS, 1 Trawniki-man
Termination of operation: 2300 hrs.
Will be continued on 26 April 1943 at 1000 hrs.

The SS and Police Fuehrer in the District of Warsaw
signed: Stroop
Brigadefuehrer and Maj.Gen. of Police
Certified Copy: SS-Sturmbannfuehrer

Copy   Teletype message
From: The SS and Police Fuehrer in the District of Warsaw
Warsaw, 28 April 1943.
Ref. No. I ab-St/Gr- 16 07 Journal No. 562/43 secret
Re: Ghetto operation
To: The Higher SS and Police Fuehrer East
SS-Obergruppenfuehrer and General of Police
Krueger - or deputy
Cracow

Progress of operation on 28 April 1943. Start 1000 hrs:

Today, 10 raiding parties were formed for combing out the whole of the Ghetto. These Raiding parties again discovered proceeding step by step, a number of dugouts, which were found to have been prepared as far ago as the middle of last year for use in the resistance, of the Jews. A total of 335 Jews were forcibly pulled out of these dugouts. Apart from these operations, we continued to cleanse the resistance center used by the Jewish military organization, situated at the borders of the Ghetto. We succeeded in shooting 10 more bandits and in arresting 9, beyond those caught yesterday, and in capturing more arms, ammunition, and military equipment. In the afternoon a battle group again was directed against a block of buildings which had already been combed out; the block was set on fire during this operation. As on previous days, masses of Jews emerged, forced out by the flames and the enormous clouds of smoke. At another point an Engineer Officer attached by the Wehrmacht to the units, with great trouble opened a dugout situated about 3 meters below ground. From this dugout, which had been ready since October of last year and was equipped with running water, toilet, and electric light, we pulled out 274 of the richest and most influential Jews. Today again we encountered very strong resistance in many places and broke it. It becomes clearer every day that we are now encountering the real terrorists and activists, because of the duration of the operation.

Result of today: 1,655 Jews caught for evacuation, of whom 110 were killed in battle.

Many more Jews were killed by the flames; moreover, Jews in an unascertainable number were destroyed by the dugouts being blown up. By the results of today the number of Jews caught or destroyed rises to 33,401 altogether. This number does not include the Jews who were killed by fire or destroyed in the dugouts.

Our strength: as on the previous day.

Our losses: 3 wounded (1 Police, 2 Waffen-SS)

Termination of operation: 2200 hrs.
Will be continued on 29 April 1943, 1000 hrs.

The SS and Police Fuehrer in the District of Warsaw
Signed: Stroop
SS-Brigadefuehrer and Majorgeneral of Police
Certified copy; SS-Sturmbannfuehrer

Copy Teletype message
From: The SS and Police Fuehrer in the District of Warsaw
Warsaw, 29 April 1943.
Ref. No. I ab-St/Gr 16 07 Journal No.566/43 secret.
Re: Ghetto Operation.
To: The Higher SS and Police Fuehrer East
SS-Obergruppenfuehrer and General of Police
Krueger - or deputy
Cracow

Progress of large-scale operation of 29 April 1943. Start 1000 hrs:
As on the previous day I formed search parties, who had the special task of searching those blocks of buildings which had been recently separated. A larger raiding party was detailed to clean a certain block of buildings (formerly the Hallmenn concern) and to burn this block down. 36 more dugouts used for habitation were discovered altogether, and from them and other hideouts and from the burning buildings 2,359 Jews were caught, of whom 106 were killed in battle.

Captured are 2 rifles, 10 pistols, 10 kilograms of explosives, and ammunition of various types.

When a large dugout was blown up, the entire building collapsed and every one of the bandits perished. In the ensuing conflagration loud detonations and darting flames showed that the building must have contained large stores of ammunition and explosives. Some sewer entrances were blown up. Two exits discovered outside the Ghetto were also made unusable by blowing them up or walling them up.

The depositions of some of the inmates of the dugouts are to the effect that these Jews have been unable to leave the dugouts for the last 10 days and that their food, etc. is now beginning to grow short because the large scale operation lasted so long. Furthermore, the Jews testify that bandits appeared at night who were Jews or Poles wearing black masks, who walled the dugouts up from the outside and admonished them not to give any signs of life, so that they could continue to live in the Ghetto when the action was finished. Some of the armaments factories are being evacuated very slowly. In several cases one gains the impression that this is done intentionally. Thus I discovered with regard to one FIRL, Schulz and Co., which I had visited on Easter Monday and then instructed to start evacuation at once and to it completed within 3 days, that up till today, Thursday, nothing had been done.

Our strength: as on the previous day.
Our losses: none.
Termination of operation at 2100 hrs.
Will be continued on 30 April 1943, 0900 hrs.
Total caught or destroyed: 35,760

The SS and Police Fuehrer in the District of Warsaw
Signed: Stroop
SS-Brigadefuehrer and Majorgeneral of Police
Certified Copy; SS-Sturmbannfuehrer

Copy Teletype Message
From: The SS and Police Fuehrer in the District of Warsaw
Warsaw, 30 April 1943.
Ref: No. I ab-St/Gr 16 07 Journal No.579/43 secret.
Re: Ghetto Operation
To: The Higher SS and Police Fuehrer East
SS-Obergruppenfuehrer and General of Police
Krueger - or deputy
Cracow

Progress of large-scale operation on 30 April 1943, start 09 00 hrs:
Combing out by search parties was continued. Although some giant blocks of buildings now are completely burned out, the Jews continue to stay in the dugouts 2 to 3 metres below ground. In many cases we are not able to discover those dugouts unless some Jew, whom have already caught, gives us a hint as to their whereabouts. Repeatedly, during the last few days, Jews have testified that some armed Jews emerge at night from hide-outs and threaten the other Jews with shooting if they give any signs of life. We were able to ascertain beyond all doubt that several dugouts had been closed from the outside by these bandits, who try to prove that they mean business. Altogether, 30 dugouts were discovered evacuated, and blown up today.

Again we caught a great number of bandits and subhumans. Apart from the bailing-out operations effected by small parties, two larger battle groups were occupied with bombing out and destroying by fire several interconnected blocks of buildings.

A total of 1599 Jews were caught today, of whom 179 were killed in battle. The sum total of Jews caught up to date thereby rises to 37,359. 3,855 Jews were loaded today. The number of Jews in possession of arms was much higher than before among the Jews caught during the last few days. Today, we again captured arms and particularly parts of German uniforms from them. The operation against Fort Traugutta did not have any positive results. In as far as we were able to discover subterranean exits, we either occupied them or blew them up. In attacking one of the blocks we had to use a gun today.

Our strength:
Used in the operation:

Police	51/133
Security Police	3/36
Waffen-SS	6/432
Engineer	2/40

Staff	3/7

Cordoning forces:

Waffen-SS	3/318
German Police	2/89
Trawniki men	200

moreover some Polish Police.

Our losses: 1 wounded (Police)
Termination of today's large-scale action: 2100 hours.
Will be continued on 1 May 1943, 0900 hours.
The SS and Police Fuehrer in the District of Warsaw
Signed: Stroop
SS-Brigadefuehrer and Majorgeneral of Police
Certified Copy: SS-Sturmbannfuehrer

Copy Teletype message
From: The SS and Police Fuehrer in the District of Warsaw
Warsaw, May 1 1943.
Ref. No. I ab-St/Gr 16 07 Journal No.583/43 secret.
Re: Ghetto Operation.
To: The Higher SS and Police Fuehrer East
SS-Obergruppenfuehrer and General of Police
Krueger - or deputy
Cracow

Progress of large scale operation on 1 May 1943, start 0900 hrs:
10 searching parties were detailed, moreover a larger battle group was detailed to comb out a certain block of buildings, with the added instruction to burn that block down. Within this block of buildings there existed a so-called armament factory which had not yet been entirely evacuated, although it had been enough time to do so. It was not exempted from the operation. [In] Today's operation a total of 1,026 Jews were caught, of whom 245 were killed, either in battle or while resisting

Moreover, a considerable number of bandits and ringleaders were also caught. In one case a Jew who had already been made ready for transport fired three shots against a 1st Lieutenant of Police, but missed his mark. All the Jews caught today were forcibly pulled out of dugouts. Not a single one gave himself up voluntarily, after his dugout had been opened. A considerable part of the Jews caught were pulled out of the sewers. We continued systematically blowing up or blocking up the sewer entrances. In one case the Engineers laid a strong concentrated charge and had to proceed to an adjoining entrance where they had something to do. In the meantime, a Jew from the sewer, removed the fuse from the concentrated charge, and appropriated the charge. In the further course of this operation, we succeeded in catching this Jew still in possession of the concentrated charge.

In order to ascertain the movements of the Jews in the night, today I used for the first time 5 scouting parties, each 1/9 strong, at irregular intervals during the night. In general, it has to be stated that our men need extraordinary diligence and energy to discover the Jews who are still in so called dugouts, caves, and in the sewerage system. It can be expected that the remainder of the Jews who formerly inhibited the Ghetto will now be caught. The sum total of Jews caught so far has risen to 38,385. Not included in this figure are those who died in the flames or in the dugouts. One patrol discovered an unascertainable number of corpses floating in a main sewer under the Ghetto. Outside of the Ghetto, in the immediate vicinity of Warsaw, the Gendarmerie has shot a total of 150 Jews who would be proved to have escaped from Warsaw.

Again we captured pistols and explosives.

Our strength: Used in operation:

Police	4/102
Waffen SS	7/350
Engineers	2/38
Engineering Emergency Service	1/6
Security Police	2/1

<u>Cordoning Units</u>

Waffen SS	300
German Police	1/71
Trawniki	250

Our losses: 1 Policeman – wounded yesterday, died from wounds.
Termination of today's large-scale action; 2200 hours.
Will be continued on 2 May 1943, 1000 hours.

The SS and Police Fuehrer in the District of Warsaw
Signed: Stroop
SS Brigadefuehrer and Majorgeneral of Police
Certified Copy: SS-Sturmbannfuehrer

Copy Teletype Message
From: The SS and Police Fuehrer in the District of Warsaw
Warsaw, 2 May 1943.
Ref. No. I ab-St/Gr-16 07 Journal No.584/43 secret.
Re: Ghetto Operation
To: The Higher SS and Police Fuehrer East
SS-Obergruppenfuehrer and General of Police
Krueger - or deputy
Cracow
Progress of the large-scale operation on 2 May 1943, start 1000 hrs:

9 raiding parties combed the whole area of the former Ghetto; moreover, a larger detachment was detailed to clean out or destroy one block of buildings grouped around the two armament enterprises Transavia and Wischnoiwski. To find the dugouts, the raiding parties took along with them some Jews caught on the previous day to act as guides. In these operations the raiding parties pulled out 944 Jews from the dugouts; 235 more Jews were shot on this occasion. When the block of buildings mentioned above was destroyed, 120 Jews were caught and numerous Jews were destroyed when they jumped from the attics to the inner courtyards, trying to escape the flames. Many more Jews perished in the flames or were destroyed when the dugouts and sewer entrances were blown up. The Jews were removed from the two armament concerns and the managers were requested to evacuate within a short time.

Altogether we caught today: 1,852 Jews.

The sum total of Jews caught thereby rises to 40,237 Jews. 27 dugouts were discovered, forcibly opened, and destroyed, arms and ammunition captured. When the external barricade was shot at and when some Jews who broke out from a sewer entrance outside the Ghetto made an attack, we suffered 7 losses, 4 Policemen and 3 Polish Policemen. The scouting parties used during the night encountered armed resistance from some Jews who under the protection of the darkness ventured to emerge from their holes and dugouts. We did not suffer losses thereby. On the other hand, a considerable number of Jews were killed or wounded in this operation.

Our Strength:
Used in operation:

German Police	3/98
Engineering Em. Service	1/6
Security Police	3/12
Engineers (Wehrmacht)	2/37

SS-Gren.	11/409
SS - Cav.	3/7
Cordoning forces	
German Police	2/9
SS-Gren.	1/300
Trawniki	200

Our losses: 4 Policemen wounded
3 Polish Policemen wounded.

Present at today's operation was the Higher SS and Police Fuehrer East, SS-Obergruppenfuehrer and General of Police Krueger.
Termination of operation: 2030 hours. Will be continued on 3 May 1943,

The SS and Police Fuehrer in the District of Warsaw
Signed: Stroop
SS-Brigadefuehrer of Police
Certified copy: SS-Sturmbannfuehrer

Copy Teletype Message
From: The SS and Police Fuehrer in the District of Warsaw
Warsaw, 3 May 1943.
Ref.No. I ab St/Gr 16 07 Journal No. 597/43 secret.
Re: large-scale Ghetto operation.
Higher SS and Police Fuehrer East
SS-Obergruppenfuehrer and General of Police
Krueger - or deputy
Cracow

Progress of large-scale operation on 3 May 19643, start 0900 hrs:
In the combing out of the former Jewish Ghetto today 19 more dugouts were discovered and the result was as follows:

Pulled out of dugouts	1,392 Jews
Shot	95
Evacuated from former armament factories	177

The sum total of Jews caught thereby rise to 41,806 Jews. In most cases the Jews offered armed resistance before they left the dugouts. We had two casualties (wounded). Some of the Jews and bandits fired pistols from both hands. Since we discovered several times today, that Jewesses had pistols concealed in their bloomers, every bandit will be ordered, from today on, to strip completely for the search. We captured among other things, one German rifle, model 98 two 08 pistols and, other calibres, also homemade hand grenades. The Jews cannot be induced to leave their dugouts until several smoke candles have been burned. According to depositions made yesterday and today, the Jews were asked during the second half of 1942 to erect air raid shelters. At that time under the camouflage of erecting air raid shelters, they began to build the dugouts which they are now inhabiting, in order to use them for an anti-Jewish operation. Some of the scouting parties used in the Ghetto were shot at last night. One casualty (wounded). These scouting parties reported that groups of armed bandits marched through the Ghetto.

Strength: as on previous day

Losses: 3 SS-men wounded

Termination of today's operation: 2100 hrs.
Will be continued on 4 May 1943, 0900 hrs.
3,019 Jews were loaded.

The SS and Police Fuehrer in the District of Warsaw
Signed: Stroop
SS Brigadefuehrer and Majorgeneral of Police
Certified copy: SS-Sturmbannfuehrer

Copy Teletype Message
From: The SS and Police Fuehrer in the District of Warsaw
Warsaw, 4 May 1943.
Ref. No. I ab-St/Gr 16 07 Journal No. 603/43 secret.
Re: Large-scale Ghetto operation.
To: The Higher SS and Police Fuehrer East
SS-Obergruppenfuehrer and General of Police
Krueger - or deputy
Cracow

Progress of large-scale operation on 4 May 1943, start 0900 hrs:
For mopping up the dugouts a raiding party was sent, 1/60 strong and reinforced by an Engineers' detachment provided by the Wehrmacht. This raiding party pulled 550 Jews out of the dugouts and killed in battle 188 Jews. Discovering the dugouts becomes more and more difficult. Often they can only be discovered by betrayal through other Jews. If the Jews are requested to leave their dugouts voluntarily, they hardly ever obey; they can only be forced to do so by the use of smoke candles.

The main forces were detailed about 1100 hours to comb out, mop up, and destroy two large blocks of buildings, containing the former firms Toebbens, Schulz and Co., and others. After these blocks had been completely cordoned off, we requested the Jews who were still within the buildings to come forward voluntarily. By this measure, we caught 456 Jews for evacuation. Not until the blocks of buildings were well aflame and were about to collapse did a further considerable number of Jews emerge, forced to do so by the flames and the smoke. Innumerable Jews whom we saw on the roofs during the conflagration perished in the flames. Others emerged from the upper stories in the last possible moment and were only able to escape death in the flames by jumping down. Today we caught a total of 2,283 Jews, of whom 204 were shot and innumerable Jews were destroyed in dugouts and in the flames. The sum total of Jews caught rises to 44,089.

As is learned from depositions made by the Jews, today we caught part of the governing body of the so-called "Party". One member of the committee which loads the gangs will be used tomorrow for mopping up some more fortified dugouts with armed Jews inside.When the armament enterprises were by no means valuable military equipment, as had been pretended, but trifles, like used furniture and their requisitioned items. We took appropriate measures against this at once.

The scouting parties who patrolled during the night in the former Ghetto again reported movements of the Jews in the burned out and destroyed streets and courtyards. In order to be better able to the Jews by surprise, the scouting parties at night tie rags and other stuff round their shoes. In skirmishes between the scouting parties and Jews, 30 Jews were shot.

We captured 1 carbine, 3 pistols, and some ammunition. During the conflagration a considerable amount of stored ammunition exploded.

Our strength:	
used in operation	
German Police	4/101
Engineering Em. Service	1/6
Security Police	2/14
Engineers	2/41
Waffen SS.	11/407

Cordoning forces:	Day	Night
German Police	2/87	1/11
Waffen-SS	25	1/300
Trawniki	200	
Polish Police	1/180	1/180

Our losses: None.

Termination of operation: 2330 hrs, will be continued on 5 May 1943, 1000 hours.

The SS and Police Fuehrer in the District of Warsaw
Signed: Stroop
SS Brigadefuehrer and Major-General of Police
Certified copy: SS-Sturmbannfuehrer

Copy   Teletype Message
From: The SS and Police Fuehrer in the District of Warsaw
Ref. No. I ab/St/Gr 16 07 Journal No. 607/43 secret.
Re: Large-scale Ghetto operation.
5 May 1943.
TO: The Higher SS and Police Fuehrer
SS-Obergruppenfuehrer and General of Police
Krueger - or deputy
Cracow

Progress of large-scale operation on 5 May 1943. Start 1000 hrs:
In the beginning of today's operations the raiding parties seemed to have less results than the proceeding days. When the operation terminated, however, quite a number of dugouts had again been discovered, owing to the tracking ability of the men and to betrayal; 40 of these dugouts were destroyed. As far as possible, the Jews in those dugouts were caught (1070 altogether). The combing out patrols shot about 126 Jews. Today again the Jews resisted in several places until they were captured. In several cases the entrances (hatches) of the dugouts were forcibly held or bolted from the inside, so that only using a strong explosive charge could we force them open and destroy the inmates. Today, we again captured arms and ammunition, including one pistol. From one enterprise still in existence (so-called Prosta) 2,850 Jews were caught for evacuation. This figure was included in the sum total reported earlier, so that only 1,070 have to be added; the present sum total therefore is 45,159.

Our strength: as on the preceding day.
Our losses: 1 SS man wounded, 1 Policeman wounded.
Sum total of losses to date: 8 dead, 55 wounded.
Termination of operation: 2200 hrs.
Will be continued on 6 May 1943, 0900 hrs.

The SS and Police Fuehrer in the District of Warsaw
Signed: Stroop
SS Brigadefuehrer and Majorgeneral of Police
Certified copy: SS-Sturmbannfuehrer

Copy Teletype message
From: The SS and Police Fuehrer in the District of Warsaw
Warsaw, 6 May 1943.
Ref. No.: I ab/St/Gr 16 07 Journal No. 614/43 secret.
Re: Ghetto large-scale operation.
TO: The Higher SS and Police Fuehrer
SS-Obergruppenfuehrer and General of Police
Krueger - or deputy
Cracow

Progress of large-scale operation on 6 May 1943, start 0930 hrs:
Today we combed especially those blocks of buildings which were destroyed by fire on 4 May 1943. Although it was hardly to be expected that any living person could still exist in those blocks, we discovered quite a number of dugouts in which a burning heat had developed. From these dugouts and from other dugouts which we discovered in other parts of the Ghetto, we pulled out 1,553 Jews. While resisting, and in a skirmish, 356 Jews were shot. In this skirmish the Jews fired from 08 pistols and other calibres and threw Polish "pineapple" hand grenades. One SS Unterscharfuehrer was wounded and a total of 47 dugouts were destroyed.

2 men of the external cordoning forces were wounded. The Jews who had broken out from the Ghetto seem to be returning now with the intention of assisting the Ghetto Jews force or liberating them. One Jew who had escaped from Lublin was caught just outside of the Ghetto wall. He was armed as follows: 1 08 pistol, ample ammunition, 2 Polish "pineapple" hand grenades. It could not be reliably ascertained so far whether the so-called "Party Directorate" of the Jews (PPR) have been caught or destroyed. We are on their traces. It is hoped that tomorrow we shall succeed in tracing down this so-called Party Directorate. In order to enable us to intercept more effectively the Jews and bandits who approach the Ghetto, covering detachments or the external barricade were shifted farther inside the Aryan part. The former miniature Ghetto "Prosta" was searched by raiding parties today. We caught some Jews who had stayed behind. The firm Toebbens was requested to evacuate this miniature Ghetto by noon on 10 May 1943. The so-called library, situated outside the Ghetto, was put at their disposal for temporary storage of their raw materials, etc.

The sum total of Jews caught so far rises to 47,068. The Polish Police take pains to deliver to my office every Jew who turns up within the city, because they are eager to win such promises as have been paid in earlier cases. The undersigned received some anonymous letters in which he was notified of the fact that some Jews are staying in the Aryan part of the city. One anonymous letter draws a parallel between Katyn and the large-scale action within the Ghetto.

Our Strength:

Used in operation:

German Police	4/101
Engineering Em. Service	1/6
Security Police	2/14
Engineers	3/72
Waffen SS	10/500

Cordoning forces:	Day	Night
German Police	2/87	1/11
Waffen SS	25	1/300
Trawniki	200	
Polish Police	1/180	1/180

Our losses:

1 Policeman dead

1 « seriously wounded

1 SS Unterscharfuehrer less seriously wounded.

Termination of operation: 2100 hours,
will be continued on 7 May 1943, 0930 hours.

The SS and Police Fuehrer in the District of Warsaw.
signed: Stroop
SS Brigadefuehrer and Majorgeneral of Police
Certified Copy: SS-Sturmbannfuehrer

Copy Teletype message
From: The SS and Police Fuehrer in the District of Warsaw
Warsaw, 7 May 1943.
Ref. No. I ab/St/Gr 16 07 Journal No. 616/43 secret
Re: Large-scale Ghetto
TO: The Higher SS and Police Fuehrer East
SS-Obergruppenfuehrer and General of Police
Krueger - or deputy
Cracow

Progress of large-scale operation on 7 May 1943, start 1000 hrs:
The combing-out parties today obtained the following results:

49 dugouts discovered. Part of the Jews were caught. A considerable, not ascertainable, number of Jews who refused to leave the dugouts and offered armed resistance were destroyed when the dugouts were blown up. Altogether

1,019 Jews were caught alive today, 255 shot.

The sum total of Jews caught so far rises to 48,342.

Today we again encountered armed resistance in several cases, whereby we lost 1 SS man (wounded). We captured 4 pistols of various calibres and some stores of ammunition. The location of the dugout used by the so-called select "Party Directorate" is now known. It is to be forced open tomorrow. The Jews testify that they emerge at night to get fresh air, since it is unbearable to stay permanently within the dugouts owing to the long duration of the operation. On the average the raiding parties shoot 30 to 50 Jews each night. From these statements it was to be inferred that a considerable number of Jews are still underground in the Ghetto. Today we blew up a concrete building which we had not been able to destroy by fire. In this operation we learned that the blowing up of a building is a very lengthy progress and takes an enormous amount of explosives. The best and only method for destroying the Jews therefore still remains the setting of fires.

Our strength: as on the preceding day.
Our losses: 1 Waffen-SS man wounded.
Termination of Operation: 2100 hours.
will be continued on 8 May 1943 1000 hours.

The SS and Police Fuehrer in the District of Warsaw
signed: Stroop
SS Brigadefuehrer and Majorgeneral of Police
Certified Copy: SS-Sturmbannfuehrer.

Copy Teletype message
From: The SS and Police Fuehrer in the District of Warsaw
Warsaw, 8 May 1943.
Ref. No. I ab St/Gr 16 07 Journal No. 624/43 secret.
Re: Large/scale Ghetto operation.
To: The Higher SS and. Police Fuehrer East
SS Obergruppenfuehrer and General of Police
Krueger - or deputy
Cracow

Progress of operation on 8 May 1943, start 1000 hours:
The whole former Ghetto was searched today by raiding parties for the remaining dugouts and Jews. As reported some days a number of subhumans, bandits, and terrorists still remain in the dugouts, where heat has become intolerable by reason of the fires. These creatures know only too well that their only choice is between remaining in hiding as long as possible or coming to the surface and trying to wound or kill off the men of the Waffen-SS, Police, and Wehrmacht who keep up the pressure against them.

We continued today the operation against the dugout of the so-called select "Party Directorat" which we had discovered yesterday, as reported in my teletype message yesterday. We succeeded in forcing open the dugout of the Party Directorate and in catching about 60 heavily armed bandits. We succeeded in catching and liquidating Deputy leader of the Jewish Military Organization "ZWZ" and his so-called Chief of Staff.

There were about 200 Jews in this dugout, of whom 60 were caught and 140 were destroyed, partly owing to the strong effect of smoke candles, and partly owing to heavy explosive charges which were laid in several places. The Jews whom we caught had already reported that innumerable Jews had been killed by the effect of the smoke-candles. The fight of the first six days was hard, but now we are able to state that we are catching those Jews and Jewesses who were the ringleaders in those days. Every time a dugout is forced open, the Jews in it offer resistance with the arms at their disposal, light machine guns, pistols, and hand grenades. Today we again caught quite a number of Jewesses who carried loaded pistols in their bloomers, with the safety catch released, Some depositions speak of 3 to 4,000 Jews who still remain in underground holes, sewers, and dugouts. The undersigned is resolved not to terminate the large-scale operation until the last Jew has been destroyed.

A total of 1,091 Jews were caught today in dugouts; about 280 Jews were shot in battle, innumerable Jews were destroyed in the 43 dugouts which were blown up. The sum total of Jews caught has risen to 40,712. Those buildings which had not yet been destroyed by fire, were set on fire today and we discovered that a few Jews were still hiding somewhere within the walls or in the staircases.

Our strength:			
Used in operation			
German Police	4/101		
Engineering Em Service	1/6		
Security Police	2/14		
Engineers	3/72		
Waffen SS	13/527		
Cordoning Forces:		Day:	Night:
German Police		1/87	1/36
Waffen SS		-	1/300
Trawniki		160	-
Polish Police		1/160	1/160

Our Losses:
2 Waffen SS dead,
2 Waffen SS wounded
1 Engineer wounded
A Policeman wounded on 7 May 1943 died today from wounds. We captured about 15 to 20 pistols of various calibres, considerable stores of ammunition for pistols and rifles, moreover a number of hand grenades, made in the former armament factories.

Termination of action; 2130 hours,
will be continued on 9 May 1943 1000 hours.

The SS and Police Fuehrer in the District of Warsaw
Signed: Stroop
SS Brigadefuehrer and Majorgeneral of Police
Certified copy: SS-Sturmbannfuehrer

Copy Teletype message
From: The SS and Police Fuehrer in the District of Warsaw
Warsaw, 9 May 1943. Ref: No. I ab/St/Gr 1607 Journal No. 625/43
Re: Large scale Ghetto operation
To: The Higher SS and Police Fuehrer East
SS Obergruppenfuehrer and General of Police
Krueger - or deputy
Cracow

Progress of large-scale operation on 9 May 1943, start 1000 hours:
The operation carried out today had the following result: The raiding parties at work today discovered 42 dugouts. From these dugouts we pulled out alive 1,037 Jews and bandits.

In battle 319 bandits and Jews were shot, moreover an uncertain number were destroyed when the dugouts were blown up.

The block of buildings which formerly contained the "Transavia" concern was destroyed by fire; in this operation we again caught a number of Jews, although this block had been combed through several times.

Again we captured some pistols and hand grenades.

Our strength
Used in operation:

German Police	4/103	
Security Police	2/12	
Engineers	2/67	
Waffen SS	13/547	
Cordoning forces:	Day	Night
German Police	1/87	1/36
Waffen SS	-	1/300
Trawniki	160	-
Polish Police	1/160	1/160

Our losses: none

The total of Jews caught up to date has risen to 51,313. Outside the former Ghetto 254 Jews and bandits were shot.

Termination of operation: 2100 hours,
will be continued on 10 May 1943, 1000 hours.
The SS and Police Fuehrer in the District of Warsaw
Signed: Stroop
SS-Brigadefuehrer and Majorgeneral of Police

Copy Teletype message
From: The SS and Police Fuehrer in the District of Warsaw
Warsaw, 10 May 1943.
Ref.No. I ab St/Gr 16 07 Journal No. 627/43 secret
Re. Large- scale Ghetto operation.
To: The Higher SS and Police Fuehrer East
SS Obergruppenfuehrer and General of Police
Krueger - or deputy
<u>Cracow</u>

Progress of large-scale action on 10 Mar 1943, start 1000 hrs:
Today raiding parties again combed out the area of the former Ghetto. As on preceding days we again pulled out of the dugouts, against all expectations, a considerable number of Jews. The resistance offered by the Jews had not weakened today. In contrast to the previous days, it seems that those members of the main body of the Jewish battle group who are still in existence and have not been destroyed have retired into the ruins still within their reach, with the intention of firing from there against our men and inflicting casualties.

Today we caught a total of 1,183 Jews alive, 187 bandits and Jews were shot. Again a not ascertainable number of Jews and bandits were destroyed in the blow-up dugouts. The total of Jews caught up to date has risen to 52,683.

Today at 0900 hours a truck drove up to a certain sewer in the so-called Prosta. Someone in the truck exploded two hand grenades, which was the signal for the bandits who were standing ready in the sewer to climb out of it. The bandits and Jews – there are always some Polish bandits among them – armed with carbines, small arms, and one machine gun, climbed into the truck and drove away in an unknown direction. The last man of the gang, who stood sentry in the sewer and had the duty of closing the sewer lid, was captured. It is he who gave the above information. He testified that most of the members of the gang, which had been divided into several battle groups, had either been killed in battle or had committed suicide because they had realized the futility of continuing the fight. The search for the truck, which was ordered at once, had no results. The bandits testified further that the Prosta is now the refuge for the still existing Jews because the Ghetto has become too hot for them. For this reason, I resolved to deal with the Prosta in the same manner as with the Ghetto, and to destroy this miniature Ghetto.

Today, we again captured small arms and some ammunition. The Security Police yesterday succeeded in capturing a workshop outside the Ghetto which manufactured 10 to 11,000 explosive charges and other ammunition.

Our Strength : as on the preceding day.
Our losses : 3 SS men wounded.
Owing to the excellent understanding between us and the Wehrmacht, the detachment of Engineers was reinforced. Moreover, a considerable amount of explosives were put at our disposal.
Termination of operation: 2200 hours,
will be continued on 11 May 1943, 0930 hours.

The SS and Police Fuehrer in the District of Warsaw
Signed: Stroop
SS Brigadefuehrer and Majorgeneral of Police
Certified copy: SS-Sturmbannfuehrer

Copy Teletype message
From: The SS and Police Fuehrer in the District of Warsaw
Warsaw, 11 May 1943.
Ref. No. I ab St/Gr. 16 07 Journal No. 629/43 secret.
Re: Ghetto large-scale operation.
To : The Higher SS rand Police Fuehrer East,
SS Obergruppenfuehrer and General of Police
Krueger - or deputy
Cracow

Progress of large-scale operation on 11 May 1943, start 0930 hours:
The scouting parties sent out last night again reported that there must still be some Jews within the dugouts, since some Jews were seen in the ruined street. The scouting parties shot 12 Jews. On the basis of these reports, today I again formed raiding parties which in combing out operations discovered, captured, and destroyed a total of 47 dugouts. Today again we caught some Jews who had taken refuge in ruins which were still protected by a roof. The Jews and bandits are still seeking this new refuge, because staying in the dugouts has become unbearable. One dugout was discovered which contained about 12 rooms equipped with plumbing, running water, and separate bathrooms for men and women. Considerable amounts of food were captured or secured, in order to make it more and more difficult for them to get necessary food.

A total of 931 Jews and bandits were caught. 53 bandits were shot. More of them perished when dugouts were blown up and when a small block of buildings was destroyed by fire. The total of Jews caught up to date has risen to 53,667. We captured several pistols, hand grenades, and ammunition.

We have not been able to smoke out the sewers systematically once more, since we are short of smoke candles. "OFK" is ready to provide new smoke candles.

Our strength
Used in operation :
German Police 6/126
Engineering. Em. Service 1/6
Security Police 2/14
Engineers 4/76
Waffen-SS 12/308

Cordoning Forces	Day	Night
German Police	1/112	1/86

Waffen-SS	-	1/130
Trawniki	160	-
Polish Police	1/160	1/160

Our Losses: 1 SS Man wounded.
Total of Losses up to date: 71 wounded, 12 dead.
Termination of today's operation: 2145 hours,
will be continued on 12 May 1943, 0930 hours.

The SS and Pollice Fuehrer in the District of Warsaw,
Signed: Stroop
SS Brigadefuehrer and Majorgeneral of Police
Certified copy: SS-Sturmbannfuehrer

Copy Teletype message
From: The SS and Police Fuehrer in the District of Warsaw,
Warsaw, 12 May 1943,
Ref No. I ab - ST/Gr 16 07 Journal No. 637/43 secret.
Re: Large-scale Ghetto operation.
To: The Higher SS and Police Fuehrer East
SS Obergruppenfuehrer and General of Police
Krueger - or deputy
Cracow

Progress of large-scale operation on 12 May 1943, start 0930 hours:
When the raiding parties combed out the area for remaining dugouts, in which Jews were hiding, they succeeded in discovering 30 dugouts. 633 Jews were pulled out of them and 133 Jews were shot. The sum total of Jews caught has risen to 54,463.

Furthermore, today the units cordoning off the miniature Ghetto were reinforced and destroyed by fire. Probably a considerable number of Jews perished in the flames, no accurate information in this regard could be obtained since the fire was still burning when darkness set in. One concrete building in the Prosta, from which Jews had been removed, was heavily damaged by blowing-up operations in order to make it impossible for the bandits to use it as a base later.

It is noteworthy that the Poles, without having been warned, took appropriate measures for protecting their window panes, etc., before the blowing up started.

The transports of Jews leaving here will be directed to T.II beginning today.

Our strength:
Used in operation:

German Police	5/126
Engineering Em. Service	1/6
Security Police	2/14
Engineers	4/74
Waffen-SS	12/508

Cordoning forces	Day	Night
German Police	1/112	1/86
Waffen-SS	-	1/300
Trawniki	160	-
Polish Police	1/160	1/160

Our losses: 1 Waffen SS man wounded.

Termination of today's operation: 2100 hours,
will be continued on 13 May 1943, 1000 hours.
The SS and Police Fuehrer in the District of Warsaw
signed: Stroop
SS-Brigadefuehrer and Majorgeneral of Police
Certified Copy: SS Sturmbannfuehrer

Copy Teletype message
From: The SS and Police Fuehrer in the District of Warsaw
Warsaw, 13 May 1943.
Ref. No. I ab/ St/Gr 16 07 Journal No. 641/43 secret.
Re: Large-scale Ghetto operation.
To : The Higher SS and Police Fuehrer East
SS Obergruppenfuehrer and General of the Police
Krueger - or deputy
Cracow

Progress of large-scale operation on 13 May 1943, start 1000 hours:
In combing out the Ghetto and the miniature Ghetto (Prosta) today we found 234 Jews. 155 Jews were shot in battle. Today it became clear that the Jews and bandits whom we are catching now belong to the so-called battle groups. All of them are young fellows and females between 18 and 25 years of age. When we captured one, a real skirmish took place, in which the Jews not only fired from 08 pistols and Polish Vis pistols, but also threw Polish "pineapple" hand grenades at the Waffen SS men. After part of the inmates of the dugout had been caught and were about to be searched, one of the females as quick as lightning put her hand under her shirt, as many others had done, and fetched from her bloomers a "pineapple" hand grenade, drew the safety-catch, threw the grenade among the men who were searching her, and jumped quickly to cover. It is only thanks to the presence of mind of the men that no casualties ensued.

The few Jews and criminals still staying in the Ghetto have for the last few days been using the hide-outs they can still find among the ruins, retiring at night into the dugouts whose location is known to them, to eat and get provisions for the next day. Lately we have been unable to extract information on the whereabouts of further dugouts from the captured Jews. The remainder of the inmates of that dugout where the skirmish took place were destroyed by using heavier explosive charges. From a Wehrmacht concern we evacuated 327 Jews today. The Jews we catch now are sent to T.II.

The total of Jews caught has risen to 55,179.

Our Strength:
used in operation
German Police 4/182
Engineering Em. Service 1/6
Security Police 2/14
Engineers 4/74

Waffen-SS 12/517

<u>Cordoning forces</u>

	Day	Night
German Police	2/137	1/87
Waffen-SS	-	1/300
Trawniki	270	-
Polish Police	1/160	1/160

Our losses: 2 Waffen SS dead
3 Waffen SS wounded 1 Policeman wounded.
The 2 Waffen SS men lost their lives in the air attack against the Ghetto.
33 dugouts were discovered and destroyed.
Booty: 6 pistols, 2 hand grenades, and some explosive charges.
Termination of today's operation 2100 hours.
will be continued on 14 May 1943, 1000 hours.

My intention is to terminate the large-scale operation on 16 May 1943 and to turn all further measures over to Police battalion 111/23, Unless ordered otherwise, I am going to submit to the conference of SS and Policefuehrers a detailed report of the operation, including an appendix containing photos.

The SS and Police Fuehrer in the District of Warsaw
signed: Stroop
SS Brigadefuehrer and Majorgeneral of Police
Certified copy: SS-Sturmbannfuehrer

Copy   Teletype message
From: The SS and Police Fuehrer in the District of Warsaw
Warsaw 14 May 1943.
Ref. No. I ab/St/G 1607 Journal No. 646/43 secret.
Re: Large-scale Ghetto operation.
To: The Higher SS and Police Fuehrer East
SS Obergruppenfuehrer and General of Police
Krueger - or deputy
Cracow

Progress of large-scale operation on 14 May 1943, start 1000 hrs:
The raiding parties formed today went to work within the areas allotted to each of them under orders to force open further dwelling dugouts and to catch the Jews. In this way a considerable number of bandits and Jews were caught, especially as some traces had been discovered during the night which were now followed up with good results. The night patrols clashed with armed bandits several times. Those bandits fired a machine gun and small arms. In this operation we had four casualties, 3 Waffen SS man and 1 Policeman. Repeatedly, shots were fired from the Aryan part against the external barricade. In the skirmishes about 30 bandits were shot and 9 Jews and bandits, members of an armed gang, were captured. One dugout was taken during the night, the Jews captured, and some pistols, among them one of 12 mm calibre, were captured. In one dugout inhabited by 100 persons, we were able to capture 2 rifles, 16 pistols, some hand grenades and incendiary appliances.

Of the bandits who resisted, some again wore German military uniform, German steel helmets, and "Knobelbecher". Apart from the carbines, we captured 60 rounds of German rifle ammunition.

One raiding party had a skirmish with a gang, 10 to 14 strong, on the roofs of a block of buildings at the border of the Ghetto (Aryan part). The bandits were destroyed; we suffered no losses.

The captured bandits repeatedly testify that still not all persons in the Ghetto have been caught. They confidently expect that the action will soon be over, and that they will then be able to continue to live in the Ghetto. Several bandits stated that they had long been in a position to kill off the leader of the action, the "General", as they call him, but that they would not do so, since they had orders to that effect to avoid the risk of a further intensification of the anti-Jewish measures.

Today again some concrete buildings in which the bandits find refuge time and again were blown up by the engineers.

In order to force the bandits in the sewers to come to the surface, 183 sewer entrances were opened at 1500 hours, and smoke candles were lowered into them at an ordered x-time; thereupon the bandits, seeking escape from what they supposed to be prison gas, crowded together in the centre of the former Ghetto, and we were able to pull them out of the sewer entrances there.

I shall come to a decision after tomorrow's operations regarding termination of the action.

Today SS Gruppenfuehrer and Lieutenant General of Waffen-SS von Herff was present during the operations.

Our strength:
Used in operation:
German Police 4/184
Engineering Em. Serv. 1/6
Security police 2/16
Engineers. 4/73
Waffen-SS 12/510

Cordoning forces	Day	Night
German Police	2/138	1/87
Waffen-SS	-	1/300
Trawniki	270	-
Polish Police	1/160	1/160

Our losses: 5 wounded, 4 Waffen SS, 1 Police

A total of 398 Jews were caught today, furthermore 154 Jews and bandits were shot in battle. The total of the Jews caught has risen to 55,731.

Booty: rifles, pistols, and munition. Further, a number of incendiary bottles (Molotov cocktails.)

Termination of action; 2115 hours,
will be continued on 15 May 1943 0900 hours.
The SS and Police Fuehrer in the District of Warsaw
signed: Stroop
SS Brigadefuehrer and Majorgeneral of Police
Certified copy: SS-Sturmbannfuehrer

Copy Teletype message
From: The SS and Police Fuehrer in the District of Warsaw
Warsaw, May 15th 1943.
Ref. No. I ab St/Gr-16 07 Journal No. 648/43 secret.
Re: Large-scale Ghetto operation,
To: The Higher SS and Police Fuehrer East
SS-Obergruppenfuehrer and General of Police
Krueger - or deputy
Cracow

Progress of large-scale operation on 15 May 1943 start 0900 hrs:
The scouting parties who patrolled the Ghetto last night reported that they encountered Jews only sporadically. In contrast to the preceding nights, they were able to shoot 6 or 7 Jews. The combing-out actions today also had little result. 29 more dugouts were discovered; but part of them were no longer inhabited. A total of 87 Jews were caught today and 67 bandits and Jews were shot in a battle. In a skirmish which developed around noon, and in which the bandits resisted by using Molotov cocktails, pistols, and home-made hand grenades, the gang was destroyed; but subsequently a Policeman was wounded by a shot through the right thigh.

A special unit once more searched the last block of buildings which was still intact in the Ghetto, and subsequently destroyed it. In the evening the chapel, mortuary, and all other buildings on the Jewish cemetery were blown up or destroyed by fire.

The sum total of Jews caught has risen to 55,885.

Our Strength:
Used in operation:

German Police	4/184		
Engineering Em. S.	1/6		
Security Police	2/16		
Engineers	4/74		
Waffen-SS	12/510		
Cordoning forces		Day	Night
German Police		2/138	1/87
Waffen-SS		-	1/300
Trawniki		270	-
Polish Police		160	160

Our losses: 1 Policeman wounded.

We captured 4 pistols of larger calibres, 1 infernal machine with fuse, 10 kilograms of explosives, and a considerable amount of ammunition.

Termination of operation: 2130 hours.
Will be continued on 16 May 1943, 1000 Hours.

I will terminate the large scale operation on 16 May 1943 at dusk, by blowing up the Synagogue, which we did not succeed in accomplishing today, and will subsequently charge Police Battalion 111/23 with continuing and completing the measures which are still necessary.

The SS and Police Fuehrer in the District of Warsaw
Signed: Stroop
SS Brigadefuehrer and Majorgeneral of Police
Certified copy: SS-Sturmbannfuehrer

Copy Teletype message
From: The SS and Police Fuehrer in the District of Warsaw
Warsaw, May 16th 1943.
Ref. No. I ab-St/Gr 16 07 Journal No. 652/43 secret.
Re: Large scale Ghetto operation,
To: The Higher SS and Police Fuehrer East
SS-Obergruppenfuehrer and General of Police
Krueger - or deputy
Cracow

Progress of large-scale operation on 16. May 1943, start 1000 hrs:
180 Jews, bandits, and subhumans were destroyed. The former Jewish quarter of Warsaw is no longer in existence. The large-scale action was terminated at 2015 hours by blowing up the Warsaw Synagogue.

The measures to be taken with regard to the established banned areas were handed over to the commander of police battalion III/23, whom I instructed carefully.

Total number of Jews dealt with 58,065, including both Jews caught and Jews whose extermination can be proved.

No losses today.

I will submit a final report to the conferrence of SS Police Fuehrer on 18 May 1943.

The SS and Police Fuehrer in the District of Warsaw,
signed: Stroop
SS-Brigade Fuehrer and Majorgeneral of Police
Certified copy: SS-Sturmbannfuehrer

Copy Teletype Message:
From: The SS and Police Fuehrer in the District of Warsaw
Warsaw 24 May 1943.
Ref.No. I ab- St/Gr 16 07 Journal No. 663/43 secret.
Re: Large-scale Ghetto operation.
Ref: Your teletype message No. 946 of 21 May 1943
To: The Higher SS and Police Fuehrer East
SS-Obergruppenfuehrer and General of Police
Krueger - or deputy
Cracow

I beg to reply to the above teletype message:

No.1: Of the total of 56,065 caught, about 7,000 were destroyed in the former Ghetto during large-scale operation. 6,929 Jews were destroyed by transporting them to T.II; the sum total of Jews destroyed is therefore 13,929. Beyond the number of 56,065 an estimated number of 5 to 6,000 Jews were destroyed by being blown up or by perishing in the flames.

No. 2: A total of 631 dugouts were destroyed.

No. 3 (booty):
7 Polish rifles, 1 Russian rifle, 1 German rifle 59 pistols of various calibres.
several 100 hand grenades, including Polish and home-made ones
a few 100 incendiary bottles,
home-made explosive charges,
infernal machines with fuses,
large amounts of explosives, ammunition for all calibres, including machine-gun ammunition.

With regard to the bag of arms one must take into consideration that in most cases we were not able to capture the arms themselves, since the Jews and bandits before they were captured threw them away into hide-outs and holes which we could not discover or find. The smoke which we had developed in the dugouts also prevented our men from discovering and capturing the arms. Since we had to blow up the dugouts at once we were not in a position to search for the arms later on.

The hand grenades, explosive charges and incendiary bottles captured were used at once against the bandits.

Furthermore, we captured:
1,240 used uniform tunics (partly equipped with medal ribbons, Iron Cross and East Medal)
600 pairs of used trousers
pieces of equipment, and German steel helmets,
100 horses, 4 of them in the former Ghetto (hearse).
We counted up to 23 May 1943: 4.4 million Zloty.
We captured moreover about 5 to 6 million Zloty, not yet, counted, a considerable amount of foreign currency, including:
$14:300 in paper
$9,200 in gold
large amounts of valuables (rings, chains, watches etc.)

No. 4:
With the exception of 8 buildings, (Police barracks, hospital and accommodations for working parties) the former Ghetto has been completely destroyed. Where blowing-up was not carried out only partition walls are still standing. But the ruins still contain enormous amounts of bricks and scrap material which could be used.

The SS and Police Fuehrer in the District of Warsaw
Signed: Stroop
SS-Brigadefuehrer and Majorgeneral of Police
Certified copy: SS-Sturmbannfuehrer

Pictorial Report
[There followed captions for 48 evidential photographs that accompanied the Report]

CERTIFICATE OF TRANSLATION OF DOCUMENT NO. 1061-PS

I, Virginia von Schon, 046318, hereby certify that I am thoroughly conversant with the English and German languages; and that the above is true and correct translation of document no. 1061-PS.

Virginia von Schon
046318.
END

Stroop was captured and tried by the US. He was sentenced to death but extradited for a second trial and death sentence in Warsaw. Before his execution he was reported as saying he felt no guilt about killing Jews. Stroop was hanged on 6 March 1952

Illustrations

The photographs are strictly copyright protected by the following archives:

Yad Vashem, Photo Archive, Jerusalem: pages 6, 11, 15, 16, 17, 20, 22, 28, 30, 31, 32 bottom, 37, 38, 39, 40, 41, 42, 43, 44, 45, 48, 50, 51, 52, 53, 54, 55, 56 top, 57, 60 bottom, 62, 63, 64, 79, 159, 160, 162 bottom, 170, 181, 194, 199, 204.

US Holocaust Museum: pages 12, 18, 98, 99, 124, 162 top, 178 bottom, 180, 201, 274

The Grodzka Gate – NN Theatre Photography Archive pages 13, 14, 19, 21, 23, 24, 25, 26, 27, 32 top, 33, 34, 35

Ghetto Fighters' House Museum Archive: pages 29 (photographer S. Artis), 56 bottom, 88 top, 155, 183, 184, 191, 198

Wiener Holocaust Library Collections: pages 58-59, 60 top, 61, 88 bottom, 89

Library of Congress/Bundesarchiv: page 49

Wikicommons: pages 46-47

Rochelle Moskowits: page 80

Acknowledgments

The Jewish Revolt is the first book to be published by the Jewish Brand and we hope that it won't be the last. Many people have put a great deal of time into the creation of this book and we would like to acknowledge their contribution:

Simon Bentley, Chair of Yad Yashem UK provided the initial funding for the translation of the book and for the photo licences. Without his involvement this book would not have come into existence. Evelynne Garbacz and Sophie Greenfield of Yad Vashem UK did an excellent job arranging the licences for the photos. Cleo Forstater researched the photos for the Yellow Star photo essay. Michael Wex wrote a very fine translation of *Yizker* and *The Jewish Revolt* text and we are delighted to have such a distinguished translator working with us.

Professor Antony Polonsky wrote two incisive introductions and Rachel Riley contributed a moving foreword. Stephen Morris designed the book and really acted as a co-publisher – giving us the benefit of his vast experience.

The front cover was designed by Julita Anulewicz. Mark Burman assisted us with his knowledge of Rachel Auerbach and the Warsaw ghetto. Simon Perry has provided us with invaluable support in PR for the Jewish Revolt. Rochelle Moskowits took the photo of the Jewish food ration and we have had the help of Toby Simpson and Torsten Jugl of the Wiener Library in accessing photos from their collection.

Shmuel Belovski transcribed the Stroop report for us and Sharon Ben Shem Da Silva provided Auerbach family photographs. Daniel Patt and the team at From Numbers to Names helped identify some of the people in the photographs that we found. Nathan Neuman's creative direction and diligent management were instrumental in the successful realization of this book.

Mark Forstater was the ideator and visionary force behind the book. His organizational skills and inspiring leadership throughout the process brought it to the world.

Together Mark Forstater and Nathan Neuman created

Yellow Star as a museum installation.

We are grateful to Claudia Rubenstein and Sarah Gluckstein for allowing us to premiere the book at Jewish Book Week.

We would like to acknowledge the ongoing support of the members of the Jewish Brand: Rabbi Harvey Belovski, Jeremy Wootliff, Baron Wasserman, Rick Senat, Neil Blair, Joshua London and Max Aaron – all have helped to bring the work of the Brand into the world.

Keep up with the Jewish Brand for more important books, audio books, films, and other important cultural works.

www.thejewishbrand.com

The Toby Press publishes fine writing
on subjects of Israel and Jewish interest.
For more information, visit www.tobypress.com.